# The Pen and the Sword

# The Pen and the Sword

## Israeli Intellectuals and
## the Making of the Nation-State

*Michael Keren*

*Westview Press*
*Boulder • San Francisco • London*

*To my children,*
*Timoret, Ely, and Carmil*

Copyright © 1989 by Westview Press, Inc.

Published in 1989 in the United States of America by Westview Press, Inc., 5500 Central Avenue, Boulder, Colorado 80301, and in the United Kingdom by Westview Press, Inc., 13 Brunswick Centre, London WC1N 1AF, England

Library of Congress Cataloging-in-Publication Data
Keren, Michael.
    The pen and the sword: Israeli intellectuals and the making of
the nation-state/Michael Keren.
        p.   cm.
    Includes index.
    ISBN 0-8133-0633-7
    1. Israel—Politics and government.   2. Intellectuals—Israel—
Political activity.   3. Israel—Intellectual life.   4. Politics and
culture—Israel.   5. Zionism—History.   I. Title.
DS126.5.K46   1989
956.94—dc19                                                       89-30917
                                                                        CIP

Printed and bound in the United States of America

(∞)    The paper used in this publication meets the requirements of the American National
        Standard for Permanence of Paper for Printed Library Materials Z39.48-1984.

10    9    8    7    6    5    4    3    2    1

# Contents

# Acknowledgments

I would like to thank the Pinhas Sapir Center for Development at Tel Aviv University for its financial support; the Labor Party Archives at Beit-Berl (especially Director Baruch Tor-Raz), the Archives of Jewish Education at Tel-Aviv University (especially Director Naava Eisin), and the Ben-Gurion Research Institute and Archives in Sde-Boker for granting me important documents; and my colleagues in the departments of political science at Tel-Aviv University and at the University of British Columbia in Vancouver, with which I was affiliated during 1986–1987, for their useful comments.

*Michael Keren*

# Chapter One

# Intellectuals and the State

———————◆———————

Nationalism, wrote George Steiner, is the venom of our age. It brought Europe to the edge of ruin, it drives the states of Asia and Africa like crazed lemmings, it leads us all to self-destruction. The earth grows too crowded to waste soil on barbed wire. This is why Steiner, an English-Jewish literary critic living in Switzerland, decided not to move to Israel. Israel had to make itself a closed fist, he claimed. No one is more tense with national feelings than an Israeli. Israel is a nation-state to the utmost degree; it lives armed to the teeth and its virtues are those of beleaguered Sparta.

Steiner added that these virtues are alien to the most radical, humane elements of the Jewish spirit. The Jewish spirit, as he saw it, is manifested in the critical humanism of the scholar. To preserve it, he thus had to "stay in the cold, outside the sanctuary of nationalism."[1] Steiner offered the Jewish intellectual a clear-cut choice: Either stay in the cold, an outsider to the national effort, and remain a critical humanist, or go to Israel and become part of the closed fist of the nation-state. It is a choice, Steiner wrote, between the "homeland" and the "text."[2]

This argument reflects a point of view that has prevailed in Jewish intellectual life since the "enlightenment" of the late eighteenth century. The enlightenment movement, associated mainly with the German-Jewish reformer Moses Mendelssohn (1729–1786),[3] called for the emancipation of ghetto-dwelling Jews in Europe. Emancipation meant their acceptance as citizens in their respective countries, a process felt to be made possible by the separation of state and church in both Christian and Jewish communities. Believing that the intertwining of state and church is an outrage to reason, and that the future belongs to the enlightened, Mendelssohn and a growing number of reformers, Jewish and non-Jewish, called upon the Jews to adapt to the cultural patterns of their non-Jewish environment.

Encouraged by political conditions supporting the cause of reason (such as the Edict of Tolerance issued in Austria in 1781, which granted Jewish children a certain measure of secular education), Jewish intellectuals ventured to prepare the cultural and educational background necessary for emancipation. Mendelssohn himself translated the Pentateuch into German in order to introduce students to the language of their enlightened neighbors and edge out Yiddish, the language hitherto in use. A Hebrew periodical entitled *Hame'assef,* first published in Königsberg in 1784, was dedicated to the ideas of enlightenment that spread throughout Europe. Scholars minimized elements of Judaism believed to be a hindrance to emancipation, such as the messianic idea, and educators launched educational establishments devoted to the philosophy that Jewish tradition was not the exclusive source of the values upon which the new generation of Jews should be nourished.[4]

After the Napoleonic Wars, as many Jews in central and western Europe emerged from the ghetto and sought emancipation in their countries of residence, the Jewish intellectual was credited as the avant-garde of emancipation. This was so because the Jews' hopes for equal rights depended on an alignment with the enlightened in the Christian community, and the intellectuals provided that link. Although after the restoration of 1815 the future no longer seemed to lie with reason but with romantic nationalism, the association between emancipation and enlightenment was maintained. Jewish hopes for integration in the social order resided in liberal movements composed of the middle class intelligentsia fighting for the reshuffling of that order. Thus, Jewish intellectuals were abundantly represented in European liberal movements as well as in many movements perceived to be devoted to enlightened causes ever since.[5]

Toward the end of the nineteenth century, some Jewish intellectuals, disenchanted with the chances for emancipation in an age of growing nationalism and having learned that antisemitism had not diminished among the "enlightened," turned to the national idea and established the Jewish national movement known as "Zionism."[6] The best known of these intellectuals was Theodor Herzl, a playwright and journalist whose 1895 pamphlet "The Jewish State"[7] became the founding document of the Zionist movement. In that pamphlet, inspired by the Dreyfus trial in Paris, Herzl called for a solution to the Jewish question through restoration of the ancient Jewish state. Herzl's vision of the Jews' emigration to the Jewish state included a call to the intellectual: "Let all who are willing to join us, fall in behind our banner and fight for our cause with voice and pen and deed."[8] Herzl offered his fellow intellectuals an important role in the new state: "The mediocre intellects which we produce so superabundantly in our middle classes will find an outlet in our first organizations, as our first technicians, officers, professors, officials, lawyers, and doctors; and thus the movement will continue in swift and smooth progression."[9]

Most Jewish intellectuals, however, perceived the association of the intellectual with nationalism as heretical as the association with the ghetto tradition. The enlightened Jewish intellectual was expected to maintain his position "on the borderline of various civilizations,"[10] where he would be prevented from reconciling himself to ideas that are nationally or religiously limited and be induced to strive for a universal weltanschauung. According to this point of view, the Jewish intellectual flourishes by being a cosmopolitan, whereas the nationalist cause constitutes a return to the ghetto and betrayal of the intellectual's mission.[11]

This point of view became famous in 1928 when Julien Benda, a French-Jewish intellectual, published *The Betrayal of the Intellectuals,* a strong objection to the association between intellect and nationalism. "Whatever their motives may have been," Benda wrote, "the great minds or the minds reputed such, by relating the whole of their value so noisily to their nation, have laboured in a direction contrary to that expected of them."[12] Benda's expectation of the intellectuals was that they engage in activity with a disinterested attitude—not bring their political passions into their work, as the modern intellectuals had. One of Benda's examples of this "betrayal" was Jewish nationalism. He wrote that in the past, when the Jews were accused in various countries of keeping to themselves and not assimilating, they responded by denying it. Now they assert this clannishness and even take pride in it.

Benda's accusations against the modern intellectual were largely addressed to his fellow Jewish intellectuals who had chosen the path of Zionism. Zionist intellectuals were indeed convinced, as Benda put it, "that their thought cannot be good, that it cannot bear good fruit, unless they remain on their native soil, unless they are not 'uprooted.'"[13] To Benda and many other Jewish intellectuals this was inconceivable. Once intellectuals associate themselves with the national movement, they no longer flourish as intellectuals nor can they function as critical humanists. The locus of truth is always extraterritorial, the argument goes, whereas nationalism, like every ideology, involves a distortion of the truth. The main source of effervescence in Jewish intellectual life is the marginality of Jewish life in the diaspora; operating under a flag of one's own clips the intellectual's mental wings.[14]

Zionist historiographers had cast doubt on the validity of this argument. They often ventured to show that intellectual work produced in separation from any social or national context is intellectually futile and politically disastrous. For example, in his pioneering studies on Russia's Jewry, published at the turn of the century,[15] Eliahu Tscherikower showed how in the mid-nineteenth century the refusal of the Russian Jewish intelligentsia to align with the needs and desires of the oppressed Jewish community under Czar Nicholas I (1825–1855) led to its total failure to assess reality. The intellectuals betrayed not only the Jewish masses but their own role as well, failing to apply critical thinking to the horrors of one of the darkest regimes in history. Their own self-interest as a tiny class of intellectuals facing a large and hostile orthodox community forced them to blindly consider the reactionary reign of the czar as "enlightened despotism" and drove them to support the government in its oppression of Jewish orthodoxy.

The oppressive measures of Nicholas's regime included confinement of Jewish residence to designated areas, mass transfers of Jews to those areas, censorship of literature, restrictions on traditional dress, and kidnapping of Jewish children to fill the military's recruitment quotas. Tscherikower described instances in which the intelligentsia not only refrained from playing a leadership role for the impoverished Jewish masses, but joined the government's crusade against their orthodox culture. In the 1830s, for example, Jewish intellectuals were active in censorship activities leading to the burning of books written by members of the Hassidic sect, who were believed to cherish their own spiritual leaders over the czar. In the 1840s Jewish intellectuals actively supported czarist educational measures perceived by the Jewish masses as a form of religious oppression.

The Jews were not the only oppressed people under Nicholas I; but although the oppression of the peasantry gave rise to radical thinking among intellectuals who identified with the peasants, the Jewish intelligentsia remained aloof. This was particularly apparent when Alexander II came to power in 1855. Alexander's reforms did not change the political and social status of the Jews, but his reign was seen by the Jewish intelligentsia as redeeming. The latter remained calm and patriotic in an era that, to Russian intellectuals aligned with the oppressed classes, served as a starting point for an opposition movement.[16]

In his introduction to *The Zionist Idea,* Arthur Hertzberg showed how the failure of Jewish intellectuals to acknowledge the new historical role played by the masses since the revolutions of 1848 led to evasive and self-contradictory thought. He criticized the philosopher Ahad Ha'am for his elitist view of the intellectual. Hertzberg claimed that an elitist approach prevented Ahad Ha'am from separating the history of the Jewish people from that of his own elite class. According to Hertzberg, Herzl, in 1896, having failed to convert Jewish magnates to his plan to settle Jews in Palestine, turned to the masses. He gloried in a feeling of instinctive rapport with them despite great cultural barriers. And his bid for support to a large and undifferentiated following made this unusual intellectual-statesman open a new chapter in modern Jewish history. On the other hand, Ahad Ha'am, Herzl's great opponent, distrusted the masses. His opposition to Herzl's "political Zionism," and his demand that cultural survival of the Jews be guaranteed first, was seen by Hertzberg as defense of the preeminence of the minority of well-born and traditional scholars dominant in the Jewish ghetto.[17]

The debate over the degree to which the Jewish intellectual ought to align with the national cause involves questions of great interest. How does the intellectual's alignment with the national movement relate to his role qua intellectual? Does it diminish his critical thinking or motivate it? Are political passions destructive to scholarly, literary, and artistic work or are they a source of inspiration? Is the locus of truth always extraterritorial? Does life on the margins of territorial society produce men of truth or, as Frederic Grünfeld called them, "prophets without honour"?[18] Does life in the ivory tower produce critical humanists or does it produce authoritarians frustrated over their lack of access to power?[19]

This book is about committed Jewish intellectuals—those who did not "stay in the cold" but instead subordinated their pen to the service of Zionism. By focusing on a community of deeply committed intellectuals, I put some of the above questions to an empirical test. And, as always, the shift from polemics to empirical investigation reveals that the truth is far more complex than it appeared.

First, the commitment of intellectuals to a national cause does not eliminate those parameters by which they are defined. The intellectual who is committed to nationalism does not cease to be what Steiner described as a "critical humanist." When he does cease to be one, the causes are found to lie in the complex relationship between intellectuals and the national movement or state; it is by no means a simple case of "homeland" versus "text." Second, the preceding relationship turns out to be variant over time and sensitive to intervening variables (war, for example) affecting the intellectual's political behavior. On this point I agree with Robert Brym's contention in *Intellectuals and Politics*[20] that only by analyzing the *shifting* social ties of intellectuals can we arrive at an adequate understanding of their politics. Third, the main explanation of the intellectual's political behavior, especially of his tendency to serve as political critic or to abandon that role, resides not in the intellectual's affiliation with the national movement but in the encounter between the national movement and the state.

This is the major argument of this book. Israel's intellectuals not only refused to become part of the "closed fist" of the nation-state but also never wholly came to terms with the establishment of the state. Committed as they were to the national cause and to independence, they were the first to sense the inevitable gap between the goals of the national movement and the reality of the new state. They also perceived the declining status of the intellectual when the national movement was replaced by the bureaucratic apparatus of the state. The hard encounter between the "committed intellectual" and the state, it will be shown, is a phenomenon going beyond Israel's boundaries and has been a major factor affecting intellectuals' political behavior in other new states.

Paradoxically, intellectuals' restlessness vis-à-vis the state seems to be typical of national movements in which struggle for political independence turns out to be successful. Frustration of a movement's goals gives rise to the intellectual as inspiring leader.[21] However, a movement's success in gaining political independence leaves a leader restless. And it is the intellectual's unease vis-à-vis the nation-state, rather than an absorption in it, that accounts for much of the intellectual's political behavior.

In moments of national crisis, significant changes in intellectuals' political behavior occur: They abandon critical humanism and tend to rationalize their state's policy. However, instead of accusing them of betraying critical humanism when they do, and relating the betrayal simply to their commitment to the national cause, one might find it useful to investigate the sociopolitical conditions encouraging or discouraging intellectuals to play a critical role within the framework of the nation-state and the sensitivity of these conditions to external crisis. Israel, a country tormented by continuous wars, provides an ideal laboratory for such an investigation.

It is not common to define the intellectual as critical humanist. This definition is challenging because it raises high expectations. The scholarly literature naturally prefers more neutral definitions of intellectuals as "men of ideas"[22] or "symbol specialists,"[23] for example). But as Edward Shils has suggested, the intellectual's preoccupation always involves "a measure of rejection."[24] It is Emile Zola crying, "*J'accuse*" during the Dreyfus affair, who serves as the standard to which intellectuals' political performance is mostly compared by others and themselves.[25] It may thus not only be legitimate but may also be useful to incorporate this standard in the definition of intellectuals.

Ralf Dahrendorf proposed to define intellectuals by the "independent and deliberate use of the word."[26] Dahrendorf wrote that we all use words—man is a creature who has the power of the word. But where this possession and use become independent and deliberate, the word is no longer simply an instrument of communication. When one begins to look at things from a distance, resistance to them is often close. Whoever acts does not speak, and the conservative is well advised never to pronounce the names of things threatening the status quo. This is a useful proposal: It allows us to distinguish between the ideologue who rationalizes sociopolitical positions[27] and the intellectual who looks at things from a distance, and adds a more universal perspective to political discourse. A universal perspective leads intellectuals to evaluate their own society by the same criteria by which other societies are evaluated. The intellectuals supporting Dreyfus do so not because they are "on his side" but because they apply a set of universal moral norms to the conduct of French society. The intellectual commenting on capital punishment before a city council differs from other citizens not in his or her views but in the tendency to consider, in addition to the community's interest, such universal issues as the role of punishment in society, the legal status of the matter in other societies, and the sanctity of life.[28] The intellectual may thus be defined as a person whose statements in a given sociopolitical context adhere to universal human values rather than to the demands of that context. Intellectuals are those who speak more or less free of constraints posed by specific political interests, who put, in Talcott Parsons's terms, "cultural considerations above social."[29]

The role of the intellectual is not confined to any occupational group. A priori, the scholar is no more of an intellectual than a barber. Whether a person is an intellectual or not depends on the degree to which that person applies universal norms to political discourse. Moreover, the same person may play the role of intellectual in some activities and the role of "citizen" in others.[30] At the same time, some occupational groups—especially writers, teachers, and scholars—are more engaged than others in what Alvin Gouldner called "context-free discourse,"[31] that is, the production and dissemination of language that is free from the immediate concerns of daily life. These groups thus are more likely to conform to Dahrendorf's model of intellectuals who "have removed themselves from the things of which they are speaking—and usually these are not things, but, say, relations of authority or valid notions of value or existing institutions—at least for the moment required to translate them deliberately and independently into words."[32] In other words, writers, teachers, and scholars, the three groups with which we are concerned in this book, may be expected, by nature of their preoccupation and traditions, to apply a universal perspective to political discourse. These groups are indeed identified with intellectual life in many societies and often develop the self-identity of an intelligentsia.[33]

The self-consciousness of an intellectual community over its social role and the political importance of that role allows us to call it an "intelligentsia." An intelligentsia is a community of intellectuals (not necessarily a group meeting face-to-face) with a strong sense of identity.[34] This sense of identity may vary over time, and no incumbents of an intelligentsia are expected to behave exactly the same way as their predecessors did. For instance, it would be wrong to presume, as some scholars do, that intellectuals are always contaminated by an "occupational disease" to oppose the social order[35] or that they have a "vested interest in social unrest."[36] Although the intelligentsia may resemble a social class when its members respond in a similar fashion to the same stimuli, the definition of intellectuals by their universalist perspective calls for some caution in this regard. As J. P. Nettl warned us, "the attempt to relate intellectuals to social institutionalization is a shotgun marriage of great therapeutic benefit to the priests but not to the doting couple."[37]

Neither is it justified to assume, as Dahrendorf did, that the intellectual buys the freedom to use independent and deliberate words by breaking with the primary ties of life such as family, church, and occupation.[38] To the contrary, intellectuals, though constituting a unique group by nature of their linguistic codes, are more often than not typical members of their society, committed to its fundamental values and sharing in its joys and sorrows. To most of them, intellectual life consists of a serious Socratic attempt to reconcile universalist thinking and parochial commitment. It is not the break from family, church, or occupation but the inability and unwillingness to do so that accounts for what Dahrendorf had otherwise rightly called, after Karl Mannheim, a dynamic synthesis "of detachment and belonging, alienation and participation, criticism and agreement."[39]

In his 1984 critique of Benda's *The Betrayal of the Intellectuals,* Michael Walzer[40] contrasted the model of the intellectual just described—one who is committed yet critical at the same time—to Benda's dualist notion of the intellectual. Benda, he said, divided the world into an ideal realm inhabited by intellectuals and a realm of reality inhabited by politicians and soldiers. Both realms are necessary to the wholeness of civilized life. Intellectuals uphold the eternal values of truth and justice, whereas politicians do what must be done for the survival and enhancement of their communities. To Benda, both Socrates and the Athenian jury acted correctly. We know intellectuals by their readiness to drink the hemlock. On the other side of this dualism, the world must be ruled by statesmen prepared to poison philosophers.

To Walzer, however, the two realms do not exist: There is no realm of absolute intellectuality—at least not one inhabited by human beings. The mark of intellectuals, wrote Walzer, is not that they are necessarily detached from real life but that they are "never blindly bound and wholly uncritical."[41] The intellectual stands somewhat to the side; he establishes a critical distance but not a large distance. "It's not a matter of living (spiritually) somewhere else, across a chasm, in a distinct and separate world; it's a matter of living *here*—and drawing a line."[42]

Israel's intelligentsia made a twofold commitment—to live "here" and to draw the line. A close look at its successes and failures in doing so throws light on the role of modern intellectuals who no longer reside in Benda's ivory tower but at the same time have not abandoned the tendency, stemming from their deliberate and independent use of the word, to cry *"J'accuse"* when necessary. This dual role is not easy. One can hardly be expected to enjoy the role of Shakespearean fool, belonging and not belonging to society at the same time. No one is born into the intelligentsia; critical humanism develops mostly as a result of one's preoccupation with the independent and deliberate word, not as a result of one's rebellious temperament. This is why intellectuals are often more reluctant to get involved in political causes than some people urge them to be.[43]

In viewing society from a universalist perspective, intellectuals abandon the public sentiment as a normative guide but do not abandon their social ties, political ambitions, or human fears. As intellectuals they may be critical, but as ordinary human beings—which they are— they may prefer the rewards that come with social conformity over the punishments inflicted upon the critic.[44]

This dilemma, by itself, may be the cause of an uncomfortable dissonance: Intellectuals know they should demonstrate against the government but prefer that others do so. They come to the conclusion that "something must be done" but wait for their colleagues to come to the same conclusion before they make a move. And when they do, they often miss the public office, research grant, or literary prize reserved for those who do not. Being a modern, self-conscious intellectual thus involves a constant dilemma between one's universalist thinking and one's parochial commitment to the national cause. The Polish philosopher Leszek Kolakowski, familiar with that dilemma from his own experience, explained it in psychological terms.[45] On the one hand, he wrote, the intellectual is forbidden to replace thinking with commitment because commitment implies that what seems wrong from the standpoint of universal criteria may be right from the perspective of supreme communal values. On the other hand, intellectuals have a tendency to violate this interdiction because they need the sense of commitment and belonging that one finds in religious or political groups.

However, an understanding of the intelligentsia's political behavior calls for more than psychological explanations. The intelligentsia's role as a social group is not wholly dependent upon the personalities of its incumbents. The degree to which intellectuals are critical or submissive also depends on traditions developed in the course of intellectual activity, determining both the ethos of their work and their relations to political authority.[46] It makes a difference whether one operates as part of an intelligentsia with an established tradition of political involvement or with one that objects to such involvement, whether the intelligentsia in one's country customarily rises against evil or refrains from protest. An analysis of the political behavior of the intelligentsia must therefore account for its traditions and the historical processes in which they took shape.

I have undertaken a study of the interplay in the Israeli intelligentsia between critical thinking and national commitment. I have followed the relationship between the intelligentsia and its sociopolitical environment throughout its three main phases—the rise of nationalism, the establishment of the sovereign state, and the challenge of war. No comprehensive overview of the Israeli intelligentsia is intended; I focus on Zionist intellectuals who were active in the revival of Jewish nationalism and the establishment of the state in its first two decades. Intellectuals of the political right, who play a very important role in Israeli politics today but whose presence was hardly noticeable before the Six Day War of 1967, are thus underrepresented in this study, as are religious-orthodox thinkers, whose concern with critical humanism was quite minimal from the start. The intellectuals discussed in this study are Zionists committed to both the national cause and to critical humanism; they represent the intellectual's dilemma in all its complexity.

In Chapter 2, I describe the role played by intellectuals in the Jewish national movement. Jewish nationalism, lacking a firm territorial base and emerging among people dispersed all over the world, was particularly dependent upon a cultural renaissance led by scholars, writers, and teachers, all of whom reveled in their role as the movement's avant-garde.

The encounter between the intellectuals and the state of Israel after its establishment in 1948 is detailed in Chapter 3. I show how each of the three groups became restless and critical when reality in the new state did not match the national movement's vision and they lost their avant-garde role.

In Chapter 4 I explore the intellectuals' difficulty in maintaining their newly acquired role as social critics in face of the challenge of war. The intellectuals' change of behavior in the Six Day War of 1967—believed to have had a significant impact on Israeli society—is discussed.

I relate, in Chapter 5, the reassertion by Israel's intellectuals of their role as social critics and the ways they pursued it from 1967 to the present. The description illuminates the challenge of war to the critical humanist. At the same time, it demonstrates that those intellectuals willing to face the challenge nevertheless are indispensable to democratic societies.

Jewish nationalism and the establishment of the state in its first two decades.

*Chapter Two*

# The Origins
# of Jewish Nationalism

Intellectuals have customarily played an important role in national movements because emphasis was placed on cultural revival in those movements.[1] Cultural nationalism is usually traced to the German philosopher Johann Gottfried Herder. At the end of the eighteenth century, Herder advanced the doctrine of a national soul (*Volkgeist*), which finds expression in the language, literature, law, and institutions of each people. The American historian William Langer saw the origins of nationalism in Herder's vision of a world where each nation would contribute, according to its particular genius, to the ultimate good of humanity. That vision, wrote Langer, was reinforced and expanded by ideas of the French Revolution, such as the importance of popular rights, political duty, and the right of every people to self-determination. Thereby the principle of nationalism was given a political turn: First identified with radicalism, it was, by 1848, identified with the constitutional liberalism of the middle classes.[2]

The emphasis on cultural revival had been considered the distinctive feature of nineteenth-century nationalism. In the twentieth century, wrote Ronald Sussex in his account of culture and nationalism in eastern Europe, we have seen many nationalist movements that were political in nature. The nineteenth-century revivals, on the other hand, were distinctly more cultural "and in a fundamental sense, more cultured."[3] Nationalists contended that people sharing a common culture have a claim to political independence in a given territory. This implied an important role for intellectuals. As suggested by Sussex, patriots in the nineteenth century are also the writers—in the person of a Korais, a Mapu, a Shevchenko, or a Mickiewicz. Their vision is sometimes practical, local, and pragmatic, other times it is messianic, combining immediate goals for national self-management with an almost cosmic feeling of destiny. These patriot-messiahs stand in a direct line of

*13*

descent from a distinguished former culture and country and lay claim to the modern land by the right of cultural inheritance.[4]

A closer look at twentieth-century nationalism reveals Sussex's view to be too narrow. The patriot-messiah's role in Asian or African nationalism is important, so are the roles played by the historian, the linguist, the educator, the poet, and others.[5] Konstantin Symmons-Symonolewicz, in his comparative analysis of nationalist movements, was right in proposing that any process of national awakening may be reduced to two concomitant collective activities, both undertaken by intellectuals: (1) the work of scholars, who "rediscover" the nation's culture and demonstrate the antiquity and the respectability of the nation by probing into its history and prehistory, and (2) the work of writers, especially poets, who give a new creative expression to the nation's distinctive individuality as a human collectivity.[6] A third category must be added: the work of teachers, who educate a new generation in light of the newly discovered national culture. I will now describe the contribution of each of these groups to national movements in general and to Jewish nationalism in particular.

## A Link with the Past

Scholarship, especially historical scholarship, is indispensable to any national movement. Historians, collecting records about their nation's past and producing narratives glorifying it, have always contributed to the rise of nationalism.[7] In his study *History—Remembered, Recovered, Invented,* Bernard Lewis doubted whether nationalist history ever had any value to the historian, but he did recognize the great contribution of nationalist history to the national movement itself. Lewis classified it as "invented" history: Nationalists embellish the past by correcting  or removing what is distasteful and replacing it with something more acceptable, encouraging, and conductive to the purpose in hand.

Nationalist history arose with the new idea of the nation as the basic political entity. At a time when most of the states of Europe were defined territorially and governed by dynastic monarchies, the new and revolutionary notion was propounded that the nation, defined by language, culture, and origin, constituted the true unit of political identity. From this it followed that any nation that had not expressed its nationhood in statehood was somehow deprived. Lewis showed the contribution of nationalist historiographers to this claim. They rejected the dynastic past, rejected the old loyalties, and even rejected the previous basis of group identity. Following the ways of the romantic age in which they lived, they presented a highly colored version of the past, hoping to encourage nationalism's new notions and destroy the old.[8]

Historians critical of nationalist history complained about its creators' tendency to invent the past in line with the aims of the national movement.[9] Hugh Trevor-Roper, for instance, showed that much of the Highland tradition of Scotland was invented: The creation of an independent Highland tradition—and the imposition of the new tradition, with its outward badges, on the whole Scottish nation—was the work of the later eighteenth and early nineteenth centuries. He revealed acts of bold forgery in which an indigenous literature as well as a new history for Celtic Scotland was created.[10] However, national movements are in need of history, not forgery. Harry Elmer Barnes demonstrated the degree to which historical writing was tied to the national idea in his impressive survey of nationalist historical writings in Europe and the United States, conducted in 1937.[11] Beginning with national historical literature of Germany in the days of humanism and the old empire, Barnes examined works (also from France, England, and other countries) that contributed to the national cause for over four centuries. The survey showed the enormous effort made—especially after the French Revolution, Napoleonic Wars, and regeneration of Prussia—to collect and glorify priceless records of the achievements from the remote pasts of several nations.

In dealing with the interrelation of nationalism and historiography, Barnes emphasized the development of an interest among Jews in their national history. The rise of Jewish nationalism was accompanied by the formation of historical societies in most leading modern states: the Société des Études Juives, founded in 1880, the Historical Commission of the Union of German-Jewish Congregations, appointed in 1885, the American-Jewish Historical Society, founded in 1892, and the English-Jewish Historical Society, created in 1895. These societies have done valuable work in compiling the sources of Jewish history and in arousing interest in its study.[12] Although Zionist historiography sometimes discarded the *Wissenschaft des Judentum,* the movement of nineteenth-century scholars associated with the German enlightenment, it is hard to imagine the rise of Jewish self-consciousness without the intellectual efforts of historians belonging to that movement, especially Heinrich Graetz. Graetz, author of the eleven-volume *History of the Jews from the Most Ancient Times to the Present,* published between 1853 and 1876, is thought to have revolutionized Jewish historical consciousness.

Shlomo Avinery claimed that Graetz's work contributed, more than any other piece of writing, to the emergence of a world view of the Jews as a nation and Jewish history as national history. For Graetz, Judaism was no longer considered an unchanging, dogmatic religious structure, as maintained by orthodoxy, nor was it conceived as a religious community merely possessing a moral and spiritual vision. To Graetz, the Jews were a nation, possessing historical continuity and undergoing change and transformation like all other nations. Graetz's scholarship assisted in the development of national self-awareness by explicating Judaism through the concrete historical behavior of the people over time.[13]

However, Graetz's work still dealt mainly with Jewish intellectual activities. It was Simon Dubnow who transformed Jewish historiography from being concerned with ideas to dealing with a concrete sociological entity.[14] Although a short version of Dubnow's magnum opus, *World History of the Jewish People from Their Origins to the Present,* can be found on many bookshelves in Israel, Dubnow's contribution was also somewhat minimized by Zionist historiography. (Avinery's collection on the intellectual origins of the Jewish state, for example, includes a chapter on Graetz but not on Dubnow.) This may be due to Dubnow's reluctance to consider immigration to Palestine the highlight of Jewish history, calling for "diaspora nationalism"[15] instead. The way the eighty-one-year-old scholar died on December 8, 1941—shot by a drunken Latvian militiaman herding the aged and feeble Jews of Riga into a waiting bus—was seen as a symbol of the failure of his call for Jewish autonomy in the diaspora. At the same time, Dubnow's contribution to the development of Jewish self-consciousness had been indispensable.

Dubnow criticized Graetz's work for dealing mainly with Jewish intellectual activities and for assuming that a people deprived of state and territory can play an active role in history only in the field of intellectual life. Dubnow proposed an alternative conception expressed in his introduction to the ten-volume *World History.*[16] Basic to this conception is the idea that Jews were at all times and in all countries the subjects and creators of their own history, not only in the intellectual sphere but also in the social sphere. Dubnow wrote that during the period of their political independence as well as their stateless period, the Jews appeared among the other nations not merely as a religious community but with the distinctive characteristics of a nation.

Dubnow was aware that this new conception of Jewish historiography was itself nourished by the development of nationalism in Europe. He explained that Jewish historiography in the past was swept along by the general current among the gentiles that concerned itself more with the religion of Judaism than with its "living creator, the Jewish people."[17] Even an opponent of this dogma like Graetz was not able to go counter to the current. However, the nationalist age brought a new conception of Jewish history, a sociological conception.

Slowly the awareness grew that the Jewish people had not been entirely absorbed all these centuries by its "thought and suffering," but that it had concerned itself with constructing its life as a separate social unit, under the most varied conditions of existence, and that, therefore, it was the foremost task of historiography to try to understand this process of building the life of the Jewish people.[18]

It is hard to measure the influence of the historian on the national movement. Historical research does not sway people, and even in the intellectual sphere—not to speak of the political—its impact is largely dependent upon philosophers, sociologists, and other scholars who interpret it. At the same time, it is impossible to think of the influential treatises of Jewish nationalists, such as the philosophical writings of Ahad Ha'am, without the historiographical base provided by Dubnow. It was from Dubnow's thorough investigation of Jewish history that the image of a Jewish nation was derived by those who pursued the national cause in the political world. His scholarship set the conditions of nationality and showed how they were fulfilled for the Jewish people. Dubnow wrote in one of his letters that a nationality, in its overall development, is a cultural-historical collectivity whose members are united originally by common descent, language, territory, and state, but who after some time reach a spiritual unity based upon a common cultural heritage, historical traditions, common spiritual and social ideals, and other characteristics of development. The Jewish nationality, which fulfills all these conditions and is conscious of its nationality, "is the highest type of cultural-historical or spiritual nation."[19]

The historian who established that the Jews were fulfilling the conditions of nationhood gave substance to the elaboration of the concept of nationhood by Zionist philosophers. The most noted among them was Ahad Ha'am, pen name for Asher Ginzberg (1856–1927), who developed the idea of Palestine as a cultural center for all dispersed Jewry.[20] Here was an intellectual par excellence, highly committed to the national idea, yet critical of its political manifestations. Political Zionism, associated with the Basel program adopted by the World Zionist Organization that was convened by Theodor Herzl in 1897, concerned itself with the search for a safe refuge for the Jewish people. Ahad Ha'am took a more comprehensive view, claiming that a movement relying on diplomacy and financial transactions makes Zionism an empty concept. He considered it the task of Zionism to create in Palestine a spiritual center that would inspire Jewish nationalism in the diaspora.

His was a spiritual Zionism: He believed the material and cultural dimensions of Jewish nationalism needed to be synthesized. In this regard, Ahad Ha'am's philosophy resembled that of other cultural nationalists such as Herder or Giuseppe Mazzini. The individual dies, he wrote,

> but the nation has a spiritual thread of life, and physical laws do not set a limit to its years or to its strength. . . . And, since it lives, it is always possible that in the course of time circumstances will enable it to live and regain strength among healthy and powerful nations, and derive substance from its intercourse with them, until at last, with the healthy blood of youth in its veins, the nation, conscious of its new strength, will become conscious also of new desires, impelling it to work actively, with body and spirit, for the future.[21]

Words like these accompany every national movement, justifying its course and defining the parameters of political action. Nationalism involves the mobilization of masses to a new idea, and the scholar elaborates and presents that idea. Ahad Ha'am played this role when he applied universal historical laws to Jewish life and thus proved the compatibility between the need for national revival and the traditional moral values of Judaism. By doing so, he set limits to Jewish nationalism, claiming that the temporary dominance of the sword over the book in the national movement should not become a way of life. Ahad Ha'am thus became a spokesman for many who felt that Jewish nationalism should not replace traditional morality with "the blare of trumpets."[22] Instead, he called for the introduction of a new current of life that "would bring a fresh life to our people, and would restore to it the faculty of moral self-development; and then, as a natural consequence, the Book, too, would develop once more."[23] Ahad Ha'am's nationalism denied that there could be inconsistency between the striving after a healthy national life and the cultivation of moral strength. To the contrary, by relating the demand for national revival to traditional morals, the scholar viewed Jewish nationalism as an evolutionary development in Jewish history rather than as an imitation of a European political current and strengthened the feeling, so crucial in national movements, of the uniqueness of the effort. To come and argue simply that we stand in need of a healthy national life like all other nations, he wrote, "is merely to bring coal to Newcastle."[24]

One of the unique features of Jewish nationalism was that it evolved among people who lacked a territorial base and were dispersed all over the world. The scholars thus had a unique task: establishing the link between the ideas of national revival and the land of Israel. The complexity of this task has recently been shown in Eliezer Schweid's study *The Land of Israel*,[25] which dealt with the Hibbat Zion movement. This movement was composed of Jewish nationalists who considered the land of Israel not as a symbol of a nation but as a national homeland and they initiated settlements there. The leaders of the new movement, wrote Schweid, set out to possess and settle the land of the fathers, and this change in goal constituted, in and of itself, a new view of the land. For many generations the Jews had viewed the land through the prism of its holiness. Now Hibbat Zion's developing ideology, which emphasized the character of the land as a national home, called for the restoration of the ancient biblical image of the land.

This required Hibbat Zion scholars to dig deeply into traditional thought in order to bring a buried layer of meaning to the surface. They had to unearth the original meaning of rabbinical texts from the thought of medieval scholars and the original significance of Scripture from the rabbinical texts. Even this, however, was insufficient. Ancient concepts concerning the ties of the people to the land had to be interpreted in the context of a modern cultural situation in which the people had their own ideas about the meaning of a homeland in their lives.

This is where the messianic idea, strongly rooted in traditional Jewish thought, played an important role.[26] Religious and secular scholars joined forces in interpreting the Jews' return to the land as "redemption." The origins of this interpretation in rabbinical scholarship can be found in the beginning of the nineteenth century with the writings of Rabbi Zvi Hirsch Kalisher and Rabbi Yehuda Hai Alkalai, who added "a praxis-oriented and slightly secular twist to the traditional messianic pious hopes and prayers."[27] The twist consisted of the idea that the temple service must be restored in Jerusalem not in some future time but right then. The rabbis, citing numerous religious authorities in the best tradition of rabbinical scholarship, claimed it was God's will that the restoration of the land, a goal for the end of days, be enhanced by action in the present. And though this was by no means their intention, their scholarship helped develop the notion, common in national movements, that the political activities of the present are endowed with God's blessing and constitute the beginning of redemption.

That tie between religious scholarship and the aims of Zionism was most firmly bound in the work of Rabbi Abraham Isaac HaKohen Kook (1865–1935), who sanctified the settlement of the land. He claimed that the Torah has more meaning in the Land of Israel. Kook, who lived in Palestine during its settlement by secular Jews, perceived the inhabitation of the land as redeeming. To him, the anticipation of redemption was the force that kept exiled Judaism alive, but "the Judaism of the land of Israel is salvation itself."[28]

Zionism's secular thinkers, most of whom were nevertheless versed in Jewish messianic thought, spoke a very similar language. The most important among them was Aharon David Gordon (1856–1922), who came to Palestine in 1904 and became the towering ideologue of the labor movement there.[29] More than any other person, Gordon is associated with the attempt to apply principles of nationalism and socialism to reality in Palestine. Other intellectuals provided the theoretical link between Jewish nationalism and socialism,[30] but Gordon's philosophical work, turned, in Tolstoyan fashion, theoretical notions into active commitments. "We, who belong to a people that has suffered more than any other," Gordon wrote, "that has been torn up from its soil, alienated from nature, yet continues vigorous; we, a nation which has not been destroyed by two thousand years of misfortune, we consider that in our aim for a complete regeneration there can be no other possibility for attaining the life we seek except to base it wholly upon its natural foundation."[31] The cornerstone of Gordon's philosophy, constructed in the tradition of romantic mysticism, was the belief in a return to nature. He considered the Jews' national renaissance unique in that it was not merely a quest for national freedom or rejuvenation but was a resurrection of the dead. Gordon thus called for a regeneration through a return to nature, creative work, a sense of order, and spiritual life. Though Gordon's approach refrained from having purely religious overtones, it was no less messianic than that of Rabbi Kook. To both thinkers, a conscious life in the land of Israel was the road to redemption.

In his study of the Zionist idea, Martin Buber acknowledged the combined contributions of Gordon, Ahad Ha'am, and Kook. The significance of the regaining of the land of Israel, he wrote, is to be understood on three levels. On the first level, associated with Gordon, it is acknowledged that the people can exist only when they are on one land together; on the second level, associatd with Ahad Ha'am, it is acknowledged that it is only on their land that the people will rediscover the free creative function of their spirit; and on the third level, associated with Rabbi Kook, it is understood that the people need the land in order to regain their holiness. The first stage, taken by itself, results in a narrow political view. The second stage by itself results in a narrow intellectual view, and the third by itself results in a narrow religious view. Buber believed that all three must be taken together if one is to understand what is meant by the rebirth of the Jewish people.[32]

It was indeed the overall effort of these thinkers and many other scholars that shaped the character of the Jewish national movement and legitimized the tie between the people and the land. But the

Jewish national movement did not benefit only from the work of giants: The tie between the people and the land was established by numerous descriptive and scientific works about the land, anthologies of ancient texts dealing with the bond between the people and the land, and of course, the beginnings of research by scientists who accompanied the settlement of the land, exploring its resources and possibilities.[33]

## The Revival of Hebrew

The tie between language and nationalism cannot be emphasized enough: A common language has always been considered one of the major traits by which a nation is defined.[34] The consideration of vernaculars as determinants of nations goes back to the philosophy of Herder, who believed that language was man's link with the past. It reveals to him the thoughts, feelings, and prejudices of past generations, which thus become deeply ingrained in his own consciousness. He, in turn, again by means of language, perpetuates and enriches these for the benefit of posterity. In this way language embodies the living manifestation of historical growth and the psychological matrix in which man's awareness of his distinctive social heritage is aroused and deepened. Herder identified those sharing a particular historical tradition grounded in language with the *Volk,* or nationality, and it was in this essentially spiritual quality that he saw the most natural and organic basis for political association.[35]

Modern scholars generally did not accept the view identifying nationality unequivocally with language. Symmons-Symonolewicz, for example, believed that this was too extreme a position. There is no doubt, he wrote, that language was generally recognized as the most fundamental distinctive trait of any European naitonality seeking emancipation and that the early leaders in the study of native languages—compilers of dictionaries and grammars, students of dialects and folklore, and others—came to be recognized, together with those who guided such nationalities politically, as the founding fathers of the nations-in-the-making. On the other hand, linguistic reform and the standardization of literary languages were undertaken at about the same time among those peoples whose national revivals came later.[36]

Also, Herder's interpreter F. M. Barnard showed that although Herder never ceased to regard the linguistic element as the decisive determinant, even he did not think of *Volk* only in the narrow linguistic sense. Herder's account of the Hebrews, in whom he sees the oldest and best example of a *Volk,* recognized additional factors determining their nationhood, such as the heritage of the land.[37] Whatever the scholarly view in this matter, however, the fact is that national movements, including that of the "Hebrews," stressed language as a necessary and sufficient condition of nationhood. The contribution of intellectuals reviving national languages, especially writers using them, was widely acknowledged in those movements.[38]

What makes national movements place such emphasis on language? Joshua Fishman, in *Language and Naitonalism*,[39] proposed three reasons. First, language provides the movement with a link to the glorious past. One of the major motivational emphases of modern nationalism has been that an ethnic past must not be lost because both the link to greatness and the substance of greatness itself can be found within it. It was on both of these accounts that the mother tongue became almost sacred, particularly for those whose current greatness was far from obvious. Second, language provides a link with authenticity. A national movement seeking a definition of the nation's "soul" can find it more readily in language than in political institutions or religion. Political fortunes wax and wane; religions are often shared with other peoples. In language, on the other hand, one has a secular symbol that can simultaneously draw upon and lean upon all of the sanctity that religion has given to texts. At the same time, it serves a new elite and a new set of goals. Third, linguistic differentiation and literary uniqueness enhance the claim of national movements to sociocultural or political independence. Without the mother tongue, Fishman stated, "it is clear that neither songs nor poems, nor slogans, nor proverbs, nor speeches, nor epics, nor books, nor schools, nor nationality, nor nation would have come into being."[40]

It is common knowledge that Jewish nationalism was closely tied to the revival of the Hebrew language. Today, it is hard to imagine the Zionist renaissance having taken place without the integrating force of biblical Hebrew and its transformation into a spoken language. In 1960, N. H. Tur-Sinai, president of Israel's Academy of the Hebrew Language, wrote, "It was both necessary and natural that the Hebrew language, the language of the Bible, and no other idiom should become the national language of Israel. It is the Hebrew Bible that represents our title-deed to the soil of Israel—and only by faithfully preserving the language of the Bible in which the land had been promised to our fathers, could we secure recognition as the legal claimants to the Holy Land."[41]

However, although it may be true that the revival of the biblical language had been functionally necessary, it was by no means "natural." To the contrary, as Tur-Sinai himself showed, the language at the end of the nineteenth century that could claim to express Jewish feelings more than any other idiom spoken by Jews was Yiddish. Yiddish, the vernacular Middle High German dialect carried by Jews to Eastern

Europe, was spoken by millions of Jews, whereas Hebrew was considered the language of scholars and priests. It would have been more natural if the language of the masses had been used to carry the messages of nationalism to them. Indeed, at the turn of the twentieth century, the founders of political Zionism were still quite unaware of the power of Hebrew as a source of national mobilization and integration. The revival of the language, and its use as a means to enhance Jewish nationalism, were largely the work of intellectuals.[42] The most noted among the intellectuals engaged in the revival of modern Hebrew was Eliezer Ben-Yehuda (1858–1922), whose zealous efforts, which resulted in the first modern Hebrew dictionary, became legendary.[43]

Born in Lithuania, Ben-Yehuda received a traditional religious education but in the typical fashion of the handful of Jewish intellectuals in that period, was exposed to scholarly and political notions of the outer society while remaining interested in Hebrew letters. He was particularly influenced by Russian populist thought that maintained that social revolution depends on the intelligentsia going down to the people. In 1879, the young Ben-Yehuda published an article along these lines. He claimed that Hebrew literature had no impact on the people, and he called upon Hebrew writers to consider the role of nationalism and to arouse the people's enthusiasm for nationalism.[44] In order to understand how revolutionary this article was, we must consider the status of the Hebrew language and Hebrew literature at the time. As noted before, the opening of ghetto walls in central Europe after the Napoleonic Wars had brought about an attempt among Jewish intellectuals to join forces with what were considered enlightened intellectual and social movements in Europe. This involved a deliberate attempt to compose works of literature in a language reflecting the spirit of enlightenment. The language that had been chosen was biblical Hebrew, which was believed to represent the Jews' authentic language and was free of linguistic dross compiled during 2,000 years of life in the ghetto.

The journal in which Ben-Yehuda's article appeared, *Hashahar,* was edited in Vienna by Peretz Smolenskin (1842–1885), who largely devoted it to an attack, along nationalist lines, on the Jewish enlightenment movement. Smolenskin considered it a corrupt and vicious movement whose sole aim was to imitate the gentiles by abandoning the strong pillars that supported the Jewish people—the hope of redemption and Jewish solidarity. The doctrine that religion is the keystone of the Jewish people, he claimed, was mere lip service by people who abandoned all hope of a life of national dignity. In addition, Smolenskin felt the goal of the enlightened was "utterly to eradicate the Hebrew language, the tongue which unites us and enables us to hear one another's cries of woe to the ends of our dispersion."[45] Ben-Yehuda concurred, but in his article and in a subsequent exchange with Smolenskin, he added an important facet to the latter's critique. Smolenskin, concerned with the destructive impact of enlightenment on the Jewish people, placed his hope in a revival of the Jewish spirit, expressed in the Torah; Ben-Yehuda had an alternative: "The land of our fathers is waiting for us; let us colonize it, and, by becoming its masters, we shall again be a people like all others."[46]

Almost two decades before Herzl published *The Jewish State,* Ben-Yehuda contended that the nation cannot live except on its own soil, and he identified the life of the nation mainly with its language. The Hebrew language, considered dead at the turn of the century, did not die of exhaustion, he claimed, "It died together with the nation, and when the nation is revived, it will live again!"[47] But Ben-Yehuda's great contribution lies in his vision that the revival of the language implied not only a scholarly effort but a practical one: "But, sir, we cannot revive it with translations; we must make it the tongue of our children, on the soil on which it once blossomed and bore ripe fruit."[48] If proof was ever needed that intellectuals' grand visions may originate from petty concerns, Ben-Yehuda provided it: Hebrew literature will renew its vigor in the holy land, he wrote, because there, with Jews becoming a majority, Hebrew writers would be able to make a living and will not be forced to write at unearthly hours.

This by itself, however, may be seen as a rather visionary statement, considering the state of the language at the time. The Hebrew Bible contains fewer than 6,000 different words and biblical Hebrew could hardly be relied on to formulate the concepts and phenomena of the modern world. This is where the intellectual became indispensable: Linguistic revival could not remain a matter of polemics but had to be conducted with skill and fervor. First of all, a vast scholarly effort was required to assemble the Hebrew vocabulary—including the biblical words—that developed throughout the generations. This included vocabulary in Talmudic literature, in loan-translations of Arabic scientific and philosophical literature in the Middle Ages, in religious poems, or in spoken dialects, such as Yiddish, incorporating Hebrew words. Then the old vocabulary had to be adapted to modern conditions and additional vocabulary had to be invented.

This is where Ben-Yehuda's proposal (in his first articles in *Hashahar*) that linguistic revival must take place on the soil to which it relates proved to be useful. His immigration to Palestine in 1881, and his fanatical activities to spread the use of Hebrew, not only contributed to its revival but also enabled him, and later his followers, to face actual linguistic and philological problems as they emerged in practical use. With Ben-Yehuda, intellectuals began to encourage the development of the language and, as the effort became more and more successful and Hebrew was put to everyday use, a feverish attempt was made to maintain scholarly standards of the language. This pattern was institutionalized with the founding of the Hebrew Language Committee in 1904. The committee called for questions concerning language use from teachers, artisans, workers, professionals, and others. It then provided an authorized vocabulary in such matters—unknown to the biblical authors—for fields such as banking and commerce, journalism, or physical education.

## The Literary Renaissance

However important scholarly activities were in the development of Hebrew as a national language, their impact might have remained quite small were it not for writers who composed literary works in Hebrew. The Zionist movement was one of the national movements blessed with a literary renaissance, which burgeoned in the twenty-five years prior to World War I.[49] This renaissance has been described as miraculous by those comparing the magnitude of the works to the status of the language at the time. A great deal of innovativeness was required: Writers were no less linguistic innovators than scholars were. Among these writers were the poets Hayim Nahman Bialik and Saul Tchernichovsky and the novelists Avraham Mapu, Mendele Mokher Seforim, Yizhak Leib Peretz, Shmuel Yosef Agnon, Yosef Hayim Brenner, and many others.[50]

It is perhaps unjust to consider these writers a "group," because they represented a variety of literary styles and concerns. Bialik's poetry is melancholic, composed by a keen observer of the hopeless decline of traditional Jewish life. Tchernichovsky, on the other hand, was a renaissance-type poet who put his faith in man and nature. Mendele (pen name for Solomon Jacob Abramowitch) was the great critic of Jewish society in the diaspora, and Agnon and Brenner provided critical insights into the life of the pioneers in Palestine. Mendele and Peretz made their literary fame in Yiddish and translated their works into Hebrew. Agnon wrote in Hebrew and is considered the greatest Hebrew writer since biblical times. These writers did, however, compose a group in the sense that their overall literary effort had accompanied and, in a very real way, motivated the Zionist movement.

Recently, the question of the origins of that literature and its influence on the growth of Jewish nationalism was taken out of the sphere of miracles and given serious scholarly attention. In an important study, David Patterson[51] analyzed the failure of the enlightenment movement's attempt, in the century following the French Revolution, to embrace the experiences of the contemporary European world in neobiblical Hebrew. It was a brave attempt but scarcely lasted thirty years: German quickly superseded Hebrew as the mode of literary expression among the enlightened.

Had modern Hebrew literature been confined to central Europe, Patterson explained, it would certainly have been short-lived. But in eastern Europe and particularly in the so-called Pale of Settlement in Russia, Hebrew literature quickly struck deep roots. The Jewish population was numerous and close knit; there was no center of cultural imitation as in Germany; and for Russian Jews there was little point in abandoning Hebrew literature and learning in favor of the inferior peasant culture that surrounded them. Consequently, Hebrew literature began to flourish, although in the beginning it was still dominated by the ideas of the enlightenment movement in Germany. For example, Avraham Mapu's novels transfer, in neobiblical Hebrew, the ideas of enlightenment into scenes from the biblical past.[52] Gradually, however, Hebrew literature came to grips with the more immediate and obvious reality of Jewish life in eastern Europe, and the two vibrant forces of the nineteenth century, nationalism and social realism, played an increasingly noticeable role.

Patterson concluded that Hebrew literature in eastern Europe, by fostering an awareness of the real nature of the Jewish situation and the decisive forces of the modern world, stimulated the growth of national consciousness and played a vital role in the process of harnessing and concentrating Jewish creativity. Both Hebrew literature and Hebrew language influenced Jewish nationalism, and both in turn were nourished by it.

Writers who moved to Palestine had an enormous impact on the Jewish community there and on their Hebrew readers abroad. The immigration of Bialik and Agnon to Palestine in the early 1920s, for instance, was not only perceived at the time as a landmark in the life of the small community, but was also taken to mark "the great transition"[53] of the Jewish cultural center from the diaspora to Palestine. Gershon Shaked, an Israeli literary scholar, claimed that in the 1920s and 1930s, the readers and writers of Hebrew literature in the diaspora expected spiritual guidance from the small Jewish community in Palestine. This community was likened by Shaked to the spiritual center Ahad Ha'am envisioned. This resemblance may be exaggerated, but in the late 1920s, Palestine began to flourish as a literary center, Hebrew became a vernacular, and conditions were created for a new code and a new frame of reference—one stressing the reality of "a new people on a new soil."[54]

At this point, however, the role of the writer in the national movement became more difficult. On the one hand he was expected—an expectation he shared—to harness his inspiration to the great social revolution taking place in Palestine. On the other hand, his qualities as a writer and his temperament as a person were often inconsistent with that expectation. The model developed whereby high demands were put on the writer that he was unable to fulfill, and his relationship with the movement came to be characterized by great ambivalence. This was particularly so in light of the prevalence of social-revolutionary ideologies in Palestine, where cultural activity was considered a major force in the mobilization of the masses toward political goals. Aharon David Gordon, the spokesman of the labor movement in Palestine, once likened the writer to "a dynamo that transforms the vital motive force that lies inert in the deepest recesses of the soul of a people and converts it into visible, concentrated energy, which gives off light and heat."[55] Labor ideologists considered writers an organic part of the national body that they were destined to lead, for they are the principal creators of national symbols—"banner-bearers of the spirit."[56]

But this role, which no social group can refuse, had a built-in difficulty. In order to meet the challenge, the writers were expected to become part of the social organism, to "live the life that is being created in all its breadth and depth with all the wealth of their talent."[57] But this form of life, one of total devotion to a firm and obligatory set of ideals, is not one in which literary talent flourishes. Even when they wished to devote themselves to the labor movement, creative writers often remained aloof and were thus considered as having betrayed their role.

On the occasion of the founding of the Writers' Association, Gordon declared that labor is the major creative force in Palestine and that this vital fact should compel the "cultural workers," as intellectuals came to be called in socialist jargon, to concern themselves most seriously with the labor movement and to understand what it required of them. What he had in mind was a relationship between writers and the labor movement that was free of "reservations or ambiguities."[58] More harmful than anything else, he contended, is "a half way measure, a compromise, a balancing between both sides, an evasion."[59] But it is reservations and ambiguities that characterize the intellectual more than absolutes and certainties. In fact, the foremost writer associated with the socialist movement in Palestine in its early days, Joseph Hayim Brenner, was all but a tormented soul and a delineator par excellence of the Jewish intelligentsia conceived not as "a new people on a new soil" but as split personalities, torn to pieces and shattered to bits in spite of their living on their own soil.

Brenner was a sharp, pessimistic observer of reality in all its dimensions—not just the revolutionary dimension. He understood the difficulty of escaping the exile-prison by ideological decision and described life in Palestine without yielding to utopian notions. No wonder Gordon considered this approach undignified. "Our self-evaluation has been and will be dependent not upon the verdict of superior intellectual judgement originating from artistic observation and aesthetic intuition. It will depend upon our own attitude to ourselves and to life, upon our demands upon ourselves and upon our powers to work."[60]

Here lay the ambivalence between the labor movement and the writers, labeled in 1934 by the movement's leader, Berl Katznelson, as "a tragic love affair."[61] Speaking at a time in which socialism had suffered great defeats in Europe, Katznelson considered the labor movement's difficulty in attracting the writers in heart and soul as tragic indeed. No other movement relied so heavily on the education of the masses, he said; the movement's ability to survive the challenge of fascism depends on a cultured working class. Katznelson and other leaders of the labor movement believed in mass mobilization through a complex system of cultural activities, such as newspapers, books, pamphlets, workers' clubs, workingmen's institutions of learning, and so on.

The intelligentsia in general and the writers in particular played a significant role in labor's political program. The intellectual's total submission to the community of workers was required. This is why the labor movement's leadership would so often mention the betrayal of the intelligentsia, referring to writers or professors at the Hebrew University (established in Jerusalem in 1925) who failed to produce works that were of direct use in the educational activities of the movement. Moreover, the labor movement's leaders were always aware that some intellectuals who harnessed their work to socialist aims— writers who presented ideal models of the pioneer, for example—were mostly second-rate intellectuals. The movement sought the support of the giants, aiming at a true integration with the cultural currents of the times.

## Pointing the Way

The absorption of teachers into the national movement followed an easier path, although the demand made upon them was no lighter. In every society teachers play an important role as the articulators and disseminators of "models of cultural order."[62] They are particularly sought after in national movements that aim for the formation of wholly new models. In their attempt to replace an old order with a new one composed of the "people," national movements, like other revolutionary movements, rely on the youth, who are supposedly uncontaminated by old traditions, and on teachers, who would show them the way.[63]

This pattern, as Hans Kohn showed in his classical studies of nationalism, was already highly developed in the French Revolution. The revolutionaries inherited, from the Age of Enlightenment, faith in the importance of education and thus established the first comprehensive system of national education. The system of education set a pattern for the future by emphasizing national authority over critical humanism. All the legislative bodies of the French Revolution agreed upon the necessity of an inclusive system of education that would raise new generations of virtuous and patriotic citizens. The educational projects the French considered included a Spartan system of education to regenerate the national spirit, a Platonic removal of children from their families to national establishments, and curricula emphasizing patriotic songs, the fundamentals of the constitution, manual labor, gymnastic exercises, and work on the soil.[64]

Teachers in the national movement were not only expected to enlighten the mind but also to instill a new morality. They were to become missionaries whose sphere of activity would encompass all spheres of life and whose work would be considered central to the development of national society. The success or failure of the movement in molding a new citizenry free of the dross of the people's religious or historical past was often attributed to the teacher. The future of the nation seemed to lie with the teacher who adhered to its values and held firm against unsupportive tendencies and behaviors, which, to be sure, the teacher is the first to identify in the classroom every morning. Although other groups of intellectuals, in spite of their political consciousness, were confined by nature of their work to the ivory tower, teachers were "out there," in direct contact with the youth, observing and reporting their progress and that of the revolution.[65]

Jewish nationalism was always influenced by the model of the biblical Exodus, according to which an old generation had to expire in the desert before a new generation, free of the norms adopted during slavery, could be relied upon to conquer the land. Similarly, after 2,000 years of Jewish life in exile, it could not be expected that the same elite who led the people in "house of bondage" would lead them successfully into the promised land. Ahad Ha'am, for example, was aware that the future of the Zionist movement lay not with the parents in the synagogues but with the children who could be influenced in educational institutions. To win over the parents, he believed, to infuse a new spirit into grown men and women who have already settled into a certain way of life, would be harder than to inspire the children,

who are a clean slate. Like many nationalist thinkers, Ahad Ha'am
relied on an avant-garde of youngsters who would adopt the values of
Zionism and spread them despite objections by their elders. To national
movements, generation gaps are desirable as long as the movement
controls the souls of the young; it is part of the dialectical process
whereby the old regime is worn out by new ideas. In the special
context of Zionism, it was to be the products of the nationalist school
against the leaders of the synagogue. "History bears witness," Ahad
Ha'am wrote, "that in a war of parents and children it is always the
children who win in the end; the future is theirs."[66]

The more that importance was attached to the work of teachers, the
more tasks they were to fulfill. If indeed the future lies with teachers,
then they must not only be totally versed in the thought and deeds
of the movement, they must be molded by its image. There was no
place for compromises—the scholar and the writer are judged by their
work, but the teacher's total being and whole personality becomes a
source of imitation for the young. Teachers must therefore play two
roles at the same time. They must be enlightened intellectuals familiar
with the treasures of universal knowledge and capable of enriching
the soul. At the same time, they cannot dwell in the ivory tower, for
they must represent the image of the new *citoyen.*

This double task was required particularly by labor ideologues. To
Gordon, the teacher as educator must be "a philosopher with a full,
individual world outlook."[67] At the same time the teacher had to be
the "son of nature."[68] Education, Gordon claimed, is not attained
through books or oral instruction. "The educator must be the book
or the living image, so that the student without any instruction from
the educator must see and realize what the educator has created and
creates of himself and of his talents."[69] There was no reason for the
teachers to object to the role attributed to them by labor ideologues.
In many societies teachers are held in low esteem; during the formative
years of the Jewish settlement in Palestine, though, teaching was an
attractive vocation and teachers occupied a high position, second only
to the pioneers in agricultural settlements.[70]

Moreover, the teachers' feeling that they were the avant-garde of the
nation was enhanced by the high degree of control they had on the
educational process. In a developing society, lacking established educational institutions and norms, the teacher was truly in charge. As
early as 1903 the Teachers' Federation was formed, becoming one of
the first social institutions of the new society. This federation played
a major role in the establishment of schools, recruitment of teachers,
development of curricula, and printing of books and newspapers. During
the British mandate constituted in Palestine after World War I, education

was placed under the control of the World Zionist Organization, a move that strengthened even more the teachers' influence over the educational process.[71]

This influence was particularly apparent in the curriculum that was always conceived to be part of the overall Zionist effort. Secular schools became "agents of Zionist education."[72] This education had many expressions: From its establishment, the secular Hebrew school in Palestine taught the Bible as history, conceiving it not as a religious text but as a source of national identification. It taught Jewish history from a point of view that considered Jewish life in the diaspora as appalling. The message was that the Jews lived humiliating lives for 2,000 years because they were uprooted from their soil. To the new generation born in Palestine, on the other hand, was attributed all the qualities a national movement gives its youngsters: They were fresh, healthy sabras, free from the dross of exile and proudly building a collective society. The curriculum in literature was almost exclusively the works of selected writers identified with the renaissance of the Hebrew language. The tie of children to the homeland and its natural environment was strengthened through hikes and outings. Add to this such rituals as the planting of trees by schoolchildren, memorial days for Zionist leaders, or a weekly symbolic contribution every child was to make to the Jewish National Fund, and the educational picture was complete.

In sum, the teachers in prestate Israel played a leading role in a revolution of Jewish education along nationalist lines. Although the educational process was organized along partisan lines—consisting of a "general trend," a "labor trend," and a "religious trend"—its overall effect was one of enthusiastic devotion to the Zionist revolution. And the teachers, like other intellectuals, reveled in their role as its avant-garde, a role that remained unquestionable until the state of Israel was established.[73]

# Chapter Three

# Encounter with
# the New State

———————◆———————

Political independence is the ultimate goal of every national movement. Yet after independence is won, intellectuals often feel a sense
of disillusionment with the reality of the new state. Reality never
matches the national movement's visions, and the intellectuals, as critical
observers, are the first to reveal that Canaan is not necessarily flowing
with milk and honey.[1] The more that intellectuals perpetuate the image
of the promised land in messianic terms, the harder the coming of
the messiah is for them. "Messianism" generally refers to the intervention
of the ahistorical in human history; intellectuals often interpret the
national movement's attempt to restore a political framework for the
Volk as messianic.[2] But political independence is always achieved after
a hard struggle, which involves compromises and difficulties that
signify—even to the most messianically oriented poet—that politics is
hardly conducted by divine intervention.[3] Many problems can come
with political independence. Self-government may not be successful
because political freedom brings new forms of oppression and corruption. The land may be divided between warring factions—the Volk
is far from being united. Political brotherhood, which characterized
the national movement as long as it fought against a common oppressor,
may be lost. Thus, throughout the world, political independence becomes a major theme in intellectuals' works, as does the contradiction
between dream and reality.[4]

Moreover, intellectuals who previously played a major role in the
national movement—who found in it, as Gouldner put it, a "historical
agent"[5] who published their work, listened to their lectures, and
rewarded their devotion—now feel useless. Scientists and professionals
are called to serve the nation-building effort, but the universalist
schemes of the scholar, writer, or teacher are pushed aside. This increases
the intellectuals' unease vis-à-vis the new state: They feel alienated

*33*

from the events taking place around them. "Those labours that fill
your days and nights," wrote Pakistan's great poet Faiz Ahmed Faiz,
"are doomed to be this time too in vain."[6] One of the strongest
expressions of intellectuals' alienation can be found in Wole Soyinka's
novel *The Interpreters*.[7] Soyinka, a Nigerian who observed his country's
quarrels and coups after independence, described a group of young
university graduates who go to night clubs, drink, attend parties, make
love, meditate on their role in society, and attack the sterility and
philistinism by which they are unhappily surrounded. In the novel
one finds not only a typical attack on the abuse of power by the new
ruling elites of Africa, but also an important comment on the intellectuals. As Lewis Nkosi put it, "their failure to even raise the right
questions, let alone to participate in ameliorative action, casts them in
the role of noisy dilettantes. Talk is all they do!"[8]

In the new state, the intellectuals' former leadership role is lost and
they feel politically impotent. They go from being part of an enthusiastic
avant-garde to being helpless observers of the social and political
scene—a scene characterized by pettiness compared to the glorious
past. And nothing is more disenchanting to intellectuals than the
transformation of their vision into a thousand petty concerns and the
metamorphosis of the national movement into a normal society composed
of, to quote Frantz Fanon, "little jingoists, taxi drivers, bakers and
bootblacks."[9] Such unease in intellectuals does not develop overnight:
It evolves over time and is strongly connected to their relationship
with political authorities. The following pattern is quite common. First,
there is a promise by political leaders that the national struggle is not
over yet (the romantic era).[10] Then comes the realization by intellectuals
that reality no longer matches the nationalist rhetoric (the realistic
era).[11] And finally, many intellectuals abandon the nationalist dogmas
altogether for the sake of cosmopolitan standards of performance amid
strong critique by those intellectuals who still cling to the dogmas
(the modernist era).[12]

This pattern was identified by Charles and Barbara Jelavich in their
study of cultural developments in the Balkans.[13] When the Balkan states
were established, the intellectuals continued to support the nation, a
stance rewarded by political leaders who patronized the cultural and
educational systems as a means of strengthening the new national
order. However, with economic development came an increasing concern
on the part of intellectuals with social problems and subsequently a
realistic rather than romantic approach to the nation-state. The next
stage involved the introduction of universal standards of cultural activity,
which replaced parochial-national ones, and the turning of attention

to general cultural currents prevailing in Europe such as impressionism, neoromanticism, and symbolism.

A similar pattern existed in various African countries after independence was achieved. There, too, the romantic notion of "Africanness"—playing an ideological role in the struggle for liberation from colonial rule—was replaced after independence by realistic social concerns and subsequently by an adherence of artists, writers, and others to universal standards of performance. Poets in particular began to consider themselves "citizens of the world, . . . inheritors of a universal tradition of art and letters and not just . . . recipients of an indigenous legacy."[14]

The Israeli case followed this pattern quite closely. When the state was proclaimed in 1948, the intellectuals welcomed it qua intellectuals. For 2,000 years, they had operated on the margins of political society, whereas at this point they gained a political frame of reference like intellectuals elsewhere. One poet expressed it: "Tragedy is a soul without a body, and comedy, a body without a soul. . . . So far we have been tragedy, an abstract soul without a body. And the state—this is the form, the body we put on."[15] The feeling that statehood endows the intellectual with a new mission and dignity was strongly encouraged by Israel's state builder and first prime minister, David Ben-Gurion.[16] Leading a state-building effort amid great difficulties, and lacking the necessary natural, financial, and other material resources necessary for the task, Ben-Gurion strongly believed in the mobilization of scientists who would provide alternative resources. He also understood that it is insufficient to mobilize scientists for specific projects: The whole intellectual community must participate in heart, soul, and deed in the state-building effort.

Moreover, like leaders of other new states, Ben-Gurion developed an ideology that stressed the messianic meaning of the state-building effort and considered the hard routines of the present as the fulfillment of the messianic vision of the Jewish people and as a restoration of a glorious biblical past.[17] The messianic ideology was particularly functional in a society composed of thousands of new immigrants to whom the Zionist ideology that led the effort meant nothing and the messianic promise "For God will save Zion, and build the cities of Judah" (Psalms 69:36) meant everything. The messianic ideology required the cooperation of the intellectuals. Thus, Ben-Gurion expected not only the scientists to harness their talent to the exploration of hidden resources but also the scholars to establish the tie between the people and their past, the teachers to disseminate national ideals, and the writers to write the epic of the times.

To Ben-Gurion, this was never mere rhetoric. In March 1949, when the War of Independence was barely over, and the state-building effort had just begun, he assembled the country's literary elite in his office to promise them that the intellectuals' contribution to the national effort was not over; in fact it was only beginning. In his public appearances, he often called upon the country's intellectuals to support the messianic vision and to give a hand to the state. And they did. In the 1950s, the intellectuals rejoiced over the attention given their trade and largely participated in the dissemination of the messianic ideology. Biblical scholars were particularly cooperative: The Book of Joshua, for instance, which deals with the conquest of Canaan, became—under Ben-Gurion's inspiration—a major preoccupation for them. Many writers composed pieces of literature dealing with the War of Independence and other nationalistic themes, and teachers were active in projects to increase "Jewish consciousness" in schools. As a result of this attention, the common phenomenon of intellectuals' dissatisfaction with the state was delayed. Even if reality in the 1950s did not always seem bright, it could be seen as part of an overall state-building effort interpreted in messianic terms. There was little cause for alienation by the intellectuals once the legendary leader of the country acknowledged their contribution and drew them into the orbit of power.

And yet, within the framework of cooperation, the intellectuals abandoned the romantic attitude for a very realistic one. They became critical of what they considered Ben-Gurion's authoritarian leadership style, his activist policies in foreign affairs, and especially his application of messianic ideals to politics.[18] Gradually, the messianic ideology fell prey to the universalist perspective of the intellectuals. The latter, however cooperative, realized that a messianic view of reality provides an easy justification of any state policy. For instance, the intellectuals could not accept the rationalization of reprisal actions conducted in the early 1950s, in which Arab civilians were killed, as acts inspired by messianic vision. And while the Sinai Campaign of 1956 was described by some poets as a "return" to Mount Sinai, others viewed such mythology with suspicion. Applying empirical, analytical frames of reference to reality, scholars exposed the ahistorical nature of Ben-Gurion's ideology. It was argued that no ideology can simply tie the present with the distant past while ignoring recent history. Ben-Gurion searched the ancient biblical past in order to find a model for modern Israel in Joshua's conquests, King David's kingdom, or in the ethics of the prophets, but the intellectuals reminded him of 2,000 years of Jewish history in the diaspora that he ignored. Intellectuals became increasingly aware of the gap between messianic rhetoric and political action. As one scholar told Ben-Gurion in 1961, the example set by the prophet Isaiah ought to be followed—there are fewer references in the Book of Isaiah to messianic vision than to social critique.[19]

The shift from romantic messianism to critical realism by the intellectuals correlated with, and possibly nourished, important economic, political, and cultural developments in Israel as it moved into its second decade. In the early 1960s, development projects began to show returns, annual GNP growth averaged about 10 percent, the annual increase in private consumption was about 9 percent, and export grew by 18 percent. Growing prosperity helped to increase investment in every branch of the economy and to absorb the influx of new immigrants whose predecessors, during the 1950s, had often been housed in tents. The security situation had also stabilized somewhat after the Sinai Campaign of 1956. The years 1957–1967 were the most peaceful Israel had known.

Politically, Ben-Gurion's successor, Levi Eshkol, who came to power in 1963, was a pragmatic politician who cared more for the state budget than for messianic schemes. During his years in office, the system of "military rule" (under which the Arab community had lived since the War of Independence) was abolished, government control of the mass media was eased, and an atmosphere of open debate prevailed in discussion clubs, conferences, and on Israeli radio. The 1960s were also an era of great development of cultural and educational institutions: Hebrew University prospered and new universities were built, the Israel Museum was opened as were experimental theaters, musical establishments, and other cultural institutions.[20]

It was in this atmosphere that a modernist attitude prevailed in cultural life—in the arts, in philosophy, and especially in literature, which had led the way. In the preceding decade of nation-building, it seemed natural to mobilize the intellectual to national tasks defined by a legendary leader, and as a result, Hebrew literature dealt almost exclusively with themes related to the War of Independence. But now a young generation of writers began to realize that a mobilized literature—whether romantic or realistic—does not meet the standards universally set for literature or at least those predominating in the Western world at the time. In a society maturing economically and politically, the demand for a national epic or a state poetry seemed ridiculous, and the consideration of literature as a means of expressing political ideas, however critical those ideas, seemed wrong. Literature was to develop in its own path, reflecting a plurality of social and ethnic trends rather than predetermined ideals.

The modernist trend was felt in other cultural spheres as well. In the early 1960s, Israeli philosophers began to explore universal themes such as "the eternal silence of Pascal's infinite spaces, Kierkegaard's

religious existentialism, and Erich Neumann's essence of evil,"[21] and
teachers were exposed to educational methods prevailing in the West,
which gave them second thoughts about the teacher as disseminator
of obligatory national values.[22] But the modernist trend did not follow
an easy path, and it involved great tension within the intelligentsia.
This was so because the intellectuals' traditions, developing within
the boundaries of a national movement, rejected the notion of cultural
activity existing for its own sake. In fact, Jewish intellectuals were
always expected to make a contribution to the community, which
served as a focal point for their work.[23] In the nineteenth century, the
national community became that focal point, and many intellectuals
had difficulty abandoning it after independence. This difficulty was
reflected in an editorial that appeared in March 1964, a few months
after Ben-Gurion's resignation, in *Moznayim,* the periodical of the
Hebrew Writers' Association. The editorial lamented that the writer
was no longer asked "to provide a handkerchief to dry up the sweat

dropping from a man's forehead, nor to remove a stone from a walker's
path."[24] Without a defined social mission, the writers felt lost.

    The adoption of modernist, cosmopolitan standards were thus ac-
companied by second thoughts among many intellectuals as well as
by conflicts between modernists and traditionalists. The latter included
mainly the old guard within the intelligentsia who continued to hold
on to the view of intellectuals and their work as having a national
mission.[25] I shall now elaborate on the evolution of unease among
writers, teachers, and scholars, a feeling that gradually came to dominate

intellectual life in Israel. The intellectuals' unease reflects their difficulty
in coming to terms with the state as a "normal," modern state, as
reality rather than as vision. That difficulty, I will show later, had far-
reaching societal consequences.

## The Writers

### Statehood and the Holy Tongue

    The revival of Hebrew as a vernacular did not diminish the reverent
attitude toward it of many intellectuals. The view of Hebrew as a
sacred tongue has deep roots in Jewish thought, especially in Jewish
mythology (kabbalah), which perceives language as a "concealment"
of the sacred.[26] The strength of this notion had not been overlooked
by those who revived the language in the age of nationalism. Zionism's
poet laureate, Hayim Nahman Bialik, wrote an article titled "Revealment
and Concealment in Language,"[27] which provided an important link
between Hebrew as a sacred and as a modern language and strongly

influenced the self-perception of writers using it. According to Bialik, the words that are employed daily by human beings—those scattered by them to the wind without much thought—originated in moments of wonder and awe. Language, he believed, contains no term so slight that the hour of its birth was not one of "powerful and awesome self-revealment, a lofty victory of the spirit."[28]

As words fall from greatness and become profane, the individual in some way remains untouched. Although a word's core is consumed and its spiritual strength is hidden, an artist has the capacity to fill the husk, or supply it constantly from his own substance, and pour his own inner light into it. This, to Bialik, was a necessary process: If the spoken word were to remain at the height of its glowing power throughout history, if the same complex of emotion and thought that became attached to it in its prime were to accompany it always, perhaps no word would have attained its particular meaning. Bialik used a biblical phrase to justify his argument: "For man shall not look on me and live" (Exodus 33:20).

This conception of language puts intellectuals in a dual role. On the one hand, as individuals concerned with words that by themselves do not penetrate the essence of things, they are merely in charge of "the assignment of names and the putting up of orderly fences around images and their associations."[29] On the other hand, they are also in touch with the other side of the barrier of language, where "behind its curtain, stripped of its husk of speech, the spirit of man wanders ceaselessly."[30] This requires that language be treated with care and attention. Intellectuals who accept Bialik's image of writers as walking "across the iron bridge of the messiah"[31] have to make sure that their feet are not touching foul waters.

But this turned out to be increasingly difficult in a modern state. Israel's intellectuals used Hebrew pedantically and ceremoniously in their works and their meetings, but its development as a spoken language was inconsistent with their requirements. This situation had already been apparent when the national movement began the settlement in Palestine, and it became a major source of disquiet after statehood. Every day linguistic innovations originated in the bureaucracy, the army, academia, the media, or the street. For intellectuals who appoint themselves guardians of high culture, the public at large becomes the enemy. This process was illustrated in a series of articles written by writer Eliezer Steinman in 1965.[32] He summarized dozens of linguistic innovations that, to him, were "cold like a railway station and grey like a barrack." Steinman, who was aware how carefully Ben-Yehuda, Bialik, and others selected every Hebrew term so that it matched its sacred origins, stood helpless in the face of an influx of such foreign-sounding words as "classificazia and improvizazia, correctivi and collectivi, activi and actuali, intensivi and intuitivi, liberali and globali and totalitari, drasti and bombasti," and so on.

To Steinman, language was more than just a means of communication: He saw it as "a guide to the nation's soul, a treasure to be guarded from its enemies." Every vineyard, he wrote, needs a fence so that it does not get ravaged by wild pigs. Steinman included almost everybody in the category of wild pigs, save for a tiny elite of intellectuals singled out as the "spiritual trustees of the master of language." Steinman realized that in every society language develops to meet the requirements of specific fields. Doctors, hunters, diamond dealers, tailors, actors, children, and thieves all develop their own dialects. But beyond this inevitable process, he felt that there exists a "general language" that represents the social conscience. This language is passed from generation to generation, preserved by those having an emotional link to it.

Not everybody can play the role of preserver, he wrote: Although a temple is accessible to everybody, only priests are truly familiar with all its entries and exits. Steinman thus appointed himself, and a handful of other intellectuals, as controllers of language and culture. Just as the tree does not trim its own leaves and the broom does not clean up the house by itself, he claimed, so language cannot be left to its own natural development—only mold and rust develop naturally. Such spiritual control over the development of Hebrew was particularly warranted because, to Steinman, the development of Hebrew was an unnatural miracle in the first place. From this perspective, it is fascinating to follow the protocols of the Academy of the Hebrew Language, the institution replacing the Hebrew Language Committee, during the years of statehood.[33] An intellectual elite was appointed by law to watch over the temple, but it failed in the face of the reality of a modern state.

The Academy was often asked to authorize Hebrew terms that had developed in the course of daily life but were not in accordance with the Academy's linguistic notions. It then had to decide whether to hold firm and risk that the terms would be used by the public anyway or authorize them and distort the purity of the language. The members were often divided between those claiming that the Academy had no choice and those who insisted that it had an educational role and should not be led by the public. Some of them hoped the Academy's legal status would help stem the influx of new terms.

Academy members felt some words were too fine to be disseminated to the public. For example, the Academy searched for a substitute for the German term *schlager,* used by the public to refer to songs known in English as "hits." The proposed Hebrew word was *ya'halom,* meaning both "hit" and "diamond." Although the Academy realized that the word had a good chance of catching on with the public, it refused to authorize the word because it did not seem right to call cheap hits by the name of a precious stone. In another instance, the panel of linguists was torn over the task of finding a Hebrew expression for "teachers' college." The word in use was *beit-midrash,* which referred to the traditional house of learning in Jewish history. But this seemed most appropriate for a rabbinical seminary, not for a regular teachers' college.

The Academy was preoccupied for several years with a 1962 proposal to modify Hebrew grammar to fit the requirements of a modern state; the heated debates reflect the difficulty in doing so. The proposal, by Professor N. H. Tur-Sinai, was to replace the complex system of unwritten vowel points with one indicating, as in English, the full vocalization of words. To justify abandoning the system used in Hebrew since biblical times, Tur-Sinai pointed out the need to express one's intent accurately and efficiently, and he was careful to note that the proposed method was employed in the Babylonian Talmud. There were many objections. Some people questioned whether Israelis, who are a minority among the Jewish people in the world, had the authority to take a step of such consequences to Jewish culture. Others felt that the reform, however efficient, constituted too great a break with the biblical past. There was fear that the Bible, which everyone agreed should continue to serve as a source of inspiration, would turn into a museum item whose language differed from the spoken one. At the same time, some Academy members realized that if the reform were authorized, only intellectuals would comply—not the general public toward whom it was oriented. By then, Hebrew had already become too dynamic a language to be affected by decisions made by the guardians of high culture. As one Academy member noted with great insight, no one would bother to replace all the traffic signs in the country.

## The Autonomy of Culture

In the early 1960s, Israeli writers joined the world's prevailing literary trends.[34] Poets such as Yehuda Amichai and Nathan Zach, writers like A. B. Yehoshua and Amos Oz, playwright Nissim Aloni, and many others were producing personal, experimental, sometimes surrealist works. This trend indicated that the mobilization of the intellectual to address national tasks was over. The mobilization had, of course, always been more metaphorical than real and had been mainly self-imposed, but it still had very real effects. The writers who published in the early 1950s—including Nathan Shacham, Moshe Shamir, Aharon Megged, and S. Yizhar—were known as the generation of the War of Independence. Their works were devoted almost exclusively to themes based on that war and the nation-building effort.[35] But now cultural activity was following new, universal standards, and writers were putting the demand for cultural autonomy at center stage. In Israel, autonomy meant, first of all, abandoning national, collective themes in favor of the individual.[36]

In 1959, a new literary journal, named *Achshav* (Now), called for a break from "any totalitarianism . . . that wants to control cultural life."[37] In the first issue, literary critic Gavriel Moked called literature that adheres to an idealized social reality a "cultural left-right."[38] He complained that Israeli literature had focused so sharply on the theme of the Jewish people's redemption that it had excluded itself from the "spiritual world of the twentieth century."[39] In this century, he claimed, no literature committed to "pseudo-messianic recipes" could flourish.[40] In the same issue, Nathan Zach published a strong attack against the poetry of Nathan Alterman. Alterman was a national institution, a poet wholly committed to the state-building process, and a close associate of Prime Minister David Ben-Gurion. Zach tried to show that Alterman's "committed" poetry was not genuine and did not express true inner feeling: The plot was solved before the poem was put on paper; a message was conveyed without arousing feelings in the reader. Alterman used words, said Zach, but they were not made to speak; there was no real drama behind the curtain of words.[41]

The notion of cultural autonomy, however, was not easy for Israeli intellectuals to accept. Literary scholar Baruch Kurzweil, who possessed enormous influence, felt that as long as Israel was engaged in state-building and national defense, its cultural activity had to respond to the national challenge. A nation that believes in its destiny, he said in 1966,[42] cannot "declare" its literature to be autonomous. He demanded that Israeli authors not only follow their personal inspirations but maintain a dialogue with their social environment as well. Kurzweil cherished the model of the Hebrew writer in the diaspora who forever had to defend his cultural creed against hostile but advanced civilizations. This tension between the author and his environment had been very fruitful and inspired literary works, such as those by Franz Kafka, which were modern in the true sense of the word. If, on the other hand, Israeli literature claimed freedom from any social mission in the name of modernity, it would lack sources of inspiration. Unless it committed itself in some way to the state and its heritage, it would be doomed to remain an insignificant literature of a small province on the eastern shore of the Mediterranean.

In a sense, Kurzweil refused to acknowledge the phenomenon of statehood. It was inconceivable to him that Jewish culture be confined to the boundaries of one state and that Jewish writers make a contribution proportional to the size of the country. His great influence on literary criticism in Israel may have stemmed from the fact that others had the same difficulty in adjusting to the new conditions. As one biographer wrote, Kurzweil always continued to search for the Weimar Republic in Ramat-Gan, the small city in which he taught.[43] He harshly criticized every attempt to write literature that diverged from the rich literary tradition produced in the diaspora. When A. B. Yehoshua first published tales mixing deep surrealism with modern political messages,[44] Kurzweil called the gifted young author an imitator and a pretender. It was clear to everybody, including Kurzweil, that these short stories indicated a new development in Israeli prose and represented a far better literature than that produced by the War of Independence generation. But Kurzweil could simply not accept as authentic anything produced in modern Israel. To him, the writers of the 1960s were disoriented imitators of modernist and existentialist fashions prevailing in New York, Paris, and Berlin, and thus guilty of "spiritual suicide." In turning to their inner selves, he wrote, they showed a lack of the national responsibility that had characterized Hebrew writers in the past.[45]

Very few writers dared object to Kurzweil, the high priest of literary criticism. One of those was Amos Oz, a young novelist who in 1966 said in response to one of Kurzweil's sermons of rage and fire that he refused to accept the designation of the "degenerated ancestor of a glorious dynasty." Oz had not lived through the glorious years of the Zionist renaissance, but he did not feel that he must therefore remain silent as Kurzweil often demanded. Living in a small, besieged country, claimed Oz, hinders no one from making a contribution to human civilization.[46] This, however, was a rather exceptional response. Many young writers in modern Israel were willing to accept the verdict that by abandoning the national epic they became a degenerated species. Poet Moshe Dor sent a message to God: "Your obedient servant, the cockroach, forges a being."[47] The life of the poet in a small state could be none but forgery and mimicry in comparison with the glorious national past. In a fashion reminiscent of Soyinka, more and more writers expressed dissatisfaction about their roles and identities. In his 1965 novel, *The Living on the Dead*, Aharon Megged described the failure of an author to complete the epic of a legendary founding father he was contracted to write and his fall into a meaningless life-style as a result of his failure.[48]

Many young poets in the 1960s became nihilists. In his poems, Dor forgot his name and lost his identity card; Zach was born from nothing and returned to nothing, with no solid ground under his feet; Israel Pinkus wondered what a ship does when it is empty, having no destination and no one waiting for it on shore; and Oded Be'eri, in a short poem, made the most heretical statement of all: "We shall not climb the mount."[49] Young Israeli poets adopted the nihilistic-rebellious attitudes prevailing in Western Europe and the United States in the 1960s,[50] and the older generation was outraged. Once a year, Gideon Katznelson would publish, in *Moznayim,* a summary of nihilistic poetry and attack it in the harshest terms. In 1961, he stressed the "motive of dirt" in that poetry.[51] A year earlier he had complained about the worshipping of dirt; now he identified a far more dangerous trend— the poet floating in the polluted stream without even worshipping it. To Katznelson and his generation, nothing could be worse than the abandonment of a social mission, however undesirable, by a poet.

When Katznelson commented on a poem about a child climbing a tree to prick God with his pocketknife, he was outraged that the child had not expressed any social, national, or human reason for the act. When he criticized a poem by Zach that repeated words in an ironic fashion ("Saul listens to music/Saul listens/ What kind of music does Saul listen to?"), Katznelson defined the situation as a zero-sum game. Either Zach was engaged in sheer juggling feats, or anything that had been considered poetry in the past must be thrown into the wastebasket. To him, poetry could not simply consist of words but had to convey a national message.[52]

The struggle between the two generations over Israeli culture generated strong reactions on both sides. Older writers considered works by their younger colleagues spurious; a typical response to this criticism might involve slogans common in Zionist epics, adapted to convey nihilistic feelings. Dor used the expression, "Let's climb up the Temple Mount" in the context of a passenger riding a night train filled with shadows, without having paid for a ticket.[53] Tuvia Ruebner opened a poem with the declaration: "I exist in order to say . . ." only to conclude it with the words: "that my predecessors' history is coal, ashes, wind."[54] However, a closer look reveals that the generation gap has been exaggerated; young Israeli writers attempted, no less than their predecessors, to link the present with the past. Yitzhak Akaviahu[55] noted that Hebrew poets from Ibn Gabirol to Bialik attempted to relate images prevailing in the secular world to those of the Old Testament. Poets such as Yehuda Amichai and Amir Gilboa did exactly the same in the 1960s.

Consider the biblical image of Jacob struggling all night with an angel. In one of Amichai's poems, Jacob reveals in the morning that he had been struggling all night with a woman.[56] Gilboa added to the struggle a horde screaming an alliterative chant, "El el Israel," as do crowds at contemporary soccer games.[57] At the time, this seemed outrageous—Katznelson, for one, considered it heretical to connect the biblical image with a vulgar phenomenon like soccer. But this consideration was an outgrowth of his objection to present reality: Soccer games were already an integral part of Gilboa's reality, which he linked to the biblical past. Gilboa in his autonomous poetry was searching for roots, but Katznelson overlooked this because, to him, no true poetry could emerge in a modern state—one supposedly devoid of vision, a world of "dirty shops, kiosks, and pharmacies."[58]

## A "World of Low Current"

In 1960, S. Yizhar made a speech before the Labor party's central committee in which he labeled the present generation in Israel the "espresso generation."[59] This term, adopted from Arthur Koestler, refers to something sharp, cheap, and superficial. It expressed Yizhar's model of young Israelis who were supposedly bored, imprisoned by material possessions, and wishing only to live in peace. This, to him, was sinful. As a member of the War of Independence generation, he yearned for "something big and strong which would come to the youth and say: this is how it should be done, which would grab it by the forelocks and compel it to do what it should."[60] Aharon Megged made a similar comment in 1964 about reality in the modern state: Everybody, from high school student to adult, senses boredom and searches for escape.[61] He lamented the lack of excitement, and he felt that the state was a poor substitute for the values lost by modern man—God, messiah, or national redemption. He searched for "a tone of high voltage in a world of low current."[62]

The more Israeli society modernized, and the more modernism prevailed in literature and the arts, the more the call for "high voltage" in social and cultural life was voiced. It consisted mainly of a demand to introduce nationalist themes in lieu of cosmopolitan ones; the latter were considered light and superficial. For instance, Nissim Aloni's important play "The Emperor's New Clothes," staged in 1962 in the best tradition of absurd theater (the national hymn was composed of familiar commercials), was labeled by one critic "cosmopolitan junk" and was felt to be out of touch with the true core of life in Israel, which was still waiting for its "redeemer" in the arts.[63] Critics claimed that Israel's theater stressed aesthetics over meaning. They felt that it was not emotionally arousing—a feeling that stemmed partly from the fact that many critics were of Russian origin, and they felt uncomfortable with Anglo-Saxon motives in the arts. Modern music was also criticized for not relating enough to "the mystical kingdom of the sounds."[64]  Every aspect of mass culture was criticized when introduced into the Jewish state: musicals, hit parades, detective stories, soccer games, even modern humor.

Many Israeli intellectuals had followed the common pattern in which yesterday's revolutionaries turn into today's conservatives.[65] The interpretation of social reality as boring and of cultural life as superficial had no objective reasons: The 1960s in Israel were by no means an era of "low current." It was an exciting period of social change and cultural modernization, but the literary elite that participated in the Zionist revolution was blind to it. This blindness was largely due to their maladjustment to the technological revolution that had begun to affect Israeli life. In meetings of teachers or writers, the scientist was often portrayed as Frankenstein, and science was compared to "the angel of death who has thousands of eyes in front and in the back."[66] The growing impact of the scientist in society was perceived as immoral.[67] The technological revolution was often seen as destroying human civilization; the intellectual was assigned the role of defending it.

For example, when Norbert Wiener's *Cybernetics*[68] was translated into Hebrew, *Moznayim* stressed Wiener's idea of entropy, interpreting it as the outgrowth of modernization. Intellectuals saw themselves as being at war with a world of modern technology, global communications, and mass culture, which ought to be steered by traditional values in order to avoid entropy.[69] The traditional values were, of course, those prevailing during the glorious years of the Zionist renaissance. Many intellectuals felt that reality in modern Israel threatened these values, and they talked about the need for spiritual redemption. In 1962, for example, the writer Yeshurun Keshet portrayed himself as living in an Augean stable, where demagogues have overpowered the spiritual leaders of the community. Following the Greek mythological image, he was yearning for Hercules to come and carry out the dung.[70] Another writer, Avraham Kariv, in a long article showing how art had been defeated by science, placed his hope in a new group of artists with healthy senses who, one day, would once again climb up the "peaks of harmony."[71]

## The Teachers

### The Bureaucratic Control of Education

The Teachers' Federation had a large degree of control over the educational process and the curriculum. After the establishment of the state, education was placed under the Ministry of Education, and the teachers became frustrated. In the Federation's meeting of 1949, Chairman David Levin argued that teachers cannot operate as civil servants; they must be partners, not servants. Fifty or sixty bureaucrats in the Ministry of Education should not command 7,000 teachers. These teachers would have to teach devotion to the homeland, which could not be done as part of the Ministry of Education. "To some extent we can, may, consider ourselves a branch of the Defense Ministry," he said.[72]

David Ben-Gurion, who held the defense portfolio, accepted the offer. He shared the teachers' perception of the educational process as devoted to the shaping of good citizens and soldiers. Speaking before the 1949 Federation meeting, he promised the teachers that the establishment of a sovereign state would open new opportunities for them. In the diaspora, he said, Jewish education was confined to the book, whereas now the educator enhanced social integration. Ben-Gurion attempted to assuage the teachers' fear of the state leviathan by defining the state of Israel as a means of socially transforming the Jewish people. The state thus demanded a special attachment and commitment from the teachers. This was consistent with the teachers' traditions; they never operated without well-defined national tasks as their focal point,[73] and Ben-Gurion offered them new challenges. However, Ben-Gurion's attempt to endow the state with high values and the teachers' willingness to cooperate introduced a difficulty that came to haunt the educational process for over a decade. On one hand, the state strengthened its control over education. In 1953 Ben-Gurion succeeded in passing a state education act that united the secular educational streams developed in the prestate years (one associated with the labor movement, the other with the General Zionist party) and subordinated religious education to the Ministry of Education as well. On the other hand, the new bureaucratic structures were endowed with normative missions derived from the jargon of national movements.

For instance, Section 2 of the State Education Act mandated that the educational process in Israel be based on "the foundations of Jewish culture and on the achievements of science, on love of the homeland and loyalty to the state and to the Jewish people." The educational system had to promote freedom, equality, tolerance, mutual assistance, and love of mankind, in addition to training in agriculture and crafts. Soon it became clear that it was easier to state these goals than to fulfill them. Fulfillment would have been difficult even if the educational goals had been defined less ambitiously. As Zvi Lam pointed out, no legislative act in a democratic society can reach consensus over the goals of education.[74] Here, however, a bureaucratic structure

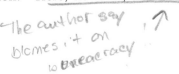
The author say blames it on bureaucracy

was asked to implement goals beyond its capacity, which led to confusion and frustration.

In 1957, Minister of Education Zalman Arranne was active in introducing a "Jewish-Israeli consciousness" program into Israeli schools. The energetic Labor leader felt that Section 2 of the State Education Act had not been implemented and that the schools' curriculum did not reflect the state's achievements. In the best tradition of bureaucracy, the norms stated in the act were translated into bureaucratic labels, and a proposal was issued that stated that the educational system had to reinforce children's identification with the Jewish heritage and their loyalty to the nation, land, state, language, and culture. In the proposal, the children were expected to be ready to sacrifice their lives for these values. Ceremonies were to be conducted during Jewish holidays, and school parties were to be held in honor of "great personalities in Israel and abroad."[75]

This action was an attempt by the state leviathan to provide ideological guidance in a fashion appropriate to a national movement but not to a modern, democratic state. In the context of statehood, there was little chance to reach consensus over the operational meaning of the norms stated in the proposal and over the exact content of such terms as "sanctity of life," "purity of soul," or "the qualities of the pioneer." No wonder the Jewish-Israeli consciousness program soon took a religious turn. Because the only norms stated in the proposal that had a clear meaning were the religious ones, the program, although it was initiated by a Labor ministry, was transformed into one disseminating religious rites and rituals in Israeli schools.[76]

How this transformation came about can be seen in the protocols of the pedagogical committee of the Teachers' Federation, which was in charge of putting the ministry's proposal into operation. In the committee's meetings, there was great confusion over the meaning of "Israeli consciousness," though everybody knew, of course, what traditional Jewish consciousness implied. Religious teachers had a great advantage over secular ones because to the former, education in Israel had to follow a well-defined road paved by tradition. The latter—who represented the vast majority of teachers in the country—could only express doubts and hesitations about the proposed curriculum.[77]

These doubts and hesitations never ended. Israeli teachers were torn by their willingness to develop "consciousness" among the youth (though they had difficulty in defining this word), their belief that the Jewish heritage ought to be preserved, their feeling that the Israeli experience demanded the formation of a new cultural heritage, and their secular life-styles and the need to familiarize their pupils with "the prayers, rites, customs, folklore, and religious symbols of Judaism."

To the Israeli teacher, the transformation from national movement to state was hard indeed.

## The Abandonment of Values

The transformation from national movement to state became even harder for the teacher when the idea was introduced that the educational process cannot, and should not, follow any one set of values as obligatory. This idea was part of the educational creed of the Western world at the time[78] and soon took hold in Israel. For a pluralistic society, it seemed unnatural to teach affirmative values, and yet, nothing was harder for teachers—especially those who participated in the Zionist renaissance—to accept. Difficult as the search for values had become, they had difficulty giving it up.

In an important article published in 1961, Aharon Kleinberger, a sociologist of education, posed the following question: Does one generation have the right to determine, through education, the nature of another generation? A society may determine the path of another generation, he claimed, only if it possesses an unquestionable set of norms. However, no such norms exist in the modern world because that world no longer believes in godly revelation, universal reason, or in the Platonic form—the sources from which man had derived the absolute status of norms in the past. The modern educator must therefore introduce pupils to a plurality of norms from which they have to  choose; no norm may be presented to them as absolute and obligatory. This is a hard task because pupils, especially adolescents, search for such norms. As proven by the tormented youth in the Western world, the abandonment of values led to disorientation. Teachers thus had a problem: They lacked well-defined norms, but they could hardly do without them.[79]

More and more academic studies revealed that a new condition prevailed in the classroom that could not be handled by the dissemination of one set of values. For example, in 1964, Hans and Shulamit Kreitler, studying the attitudes of young Israelis toward social ideals, found that ideals such as socialism that were part of the Zionist ethos were less cherished by the youth than those relating to the modern state—peace with the Arabs, security, economic independence, and democracy, for example. In an open questionnaire, the respondents noted their ideals in terms such as "conquest of nature," which were more closely linked to the welfare of humanity than to the Zionist renaissance.[80]

Another study by two sociologists looked into the dissemination of values in new immigrants' schools. It found that the traditional value system of the prestate era did not serve as a source of identification for the experimental group of new immigrants or, for that matter, for the control group of Israeli-born youth. The value of "hard work" for its own sake, for instance, appeared very low on the scale; when asked whether a youngster who won a large amount of money in a lottery should go on working, most respondents agreed that he should—otherwise he might run out of money. The researchers claimed that a new cluster of values was forming in schools—one characterized by an instrumental rather than ideological approach to life—and called upon the educators to adapt to the new conditions.[81]

Teachers who participated in the Zionist renaissance were frustrated about these findings. These teachers, facing the youth of an independent Jewish state for the first time, were charged with disseminating a set of norms with devotion and enthusiasm. They learned from academic studies, if not from personal experience, that the youth were simply too varied, lively, and pragmatic to be affected by their norms. The teachers' response was fascinating—they turned against the youth. The youth, whom they saw every morning in the classroom, became the source of all evil in the modern state. The young people seemed normless and misguided because the educational process had abandoned its traditional adherence to values.

In Israeli schools and universities of the 1960s, a new generation arose that resembled young people in other enlightened societies. They grew up in an independent state, never fought a war, enjoyed a reasonable standard of living, and were open to developments in the Western world—science, liberal democracy, and for better or worse, the youth culture. But many teachers could only interpret the situation as a value crisis, and they accused the youth of materialism and shallowness. In 1960, a "pedagogical conference" was called by the Teachers' Federation to discuss the value crisis.[82] The Federation's chairman, Shalom Levin, claimed in his opening statement that teachers had lost their sense of direction. Education that is oriented only toward the increase of knowledge leads to "cruelty, corruption, distortion and perversion of justice," he said.[83] The conference's keynote speaker, philosopher Hugo Bergman, defined the major goal of the educational process as the development of the personality. This idea was not accepted by the teachers, however. They believed the educational process should be aimed at "total identification with the nation."[84] Every important national event, such as the immigration of one hundred Jews to Israel, must be somehow noted in the classroom, one teacher said.

At the end of the second day of the conference, the teachers were glad to find out that they agreed on the values that ought to prevail in the educational process, but they longed for a time past when others

did so too. They felt that their vision of education was not shared by
their pupils' parents or by others in their social environment. One
teacher, Yaacov Amora'i, told a moving story that showed their isolation.
In 1919, his father was carried away by the Denikin militias in Russia.
His last words to his elder son were, "Who knows if I shall be back,
Yaacov—you will become a teacher and read like a Jew." Everybody
present, said Amora'i, understood what the mission consisted of, whereas
today no one would have known. People do not know what is required
of them—what it means to be a Jew.

## The Scholars

### The "New Class" and Political Power

In *Israeli Society,* Israel's foremost sociologist, S. N. Eisenstadt, wrote
that the state, seen at first as the realization of long-standing historical
aspirations, became in 1948 the fullest manifestation of the values of
Zionism, and sentiments of identification that focused on prestate
movements were transferred to the state. In many literary, journalistic,
artistic, and scientific circles, the formation of the state became a historic
event and, although there were some Byzantine sycophants, most made
an honest effort to understand this great event, participate in it, and
find ways in which to define it and make it meaningful.[85] The state
lay at the core of Eisenstadt's own sociological studies. He praised
modernization carried out by a strong and wise bureaucracy, and he
claimed that a "differentiated political system" enlarges the scope and
policies as well as the administrative services that are provided to
various groups in society. The variety of political demands that a system
can absorb, he wrote, increases with bureaucratic differentiation, and
the main condition for the maintenance of service-oriented bureaucracy
was, to him, "some basic unitary political framework."[86]

This is not to say that sociology, or for that matter any other form
of scholarship, played an explicit ideological role in the early years
of statehood. It had, however, played a role in Ben-Gurion's policy of
statism, which consisted of strengthening bureaucratic control over
functions previously performed by voluntary, partisan associations.
Moreover, many forms of scholarship that were previously ignored now
came to the fore. Sociologists, formerly disregarded by a socialist
ideology, were now called to contribute their expertise toward the
absorption of immigrants, the planning of development towns, and so
on.[87] The scientist, the academic, and the professional, treated with
ambivalence in the past, were needed in the state-building process.[88]
Because this process had been endowed with a messianic meaning,

the archaeologist, the biblical scholar, and the historian could also feel part of the "new class" of intellectuals whose services were deemed necessary in the formation of the state.[89]

The emergence of a new class in Israel in the 1950s was noted by political scientists. Peter Medding wrote in *Mapai in Israel* that the new state bureaucracies needed advanced professional and technical skills to carry out the many new tasks among the vastly increased population. Industrial, technological, and military development brought to the fore professional groups less significant before 1948, such as scientists and engineers. The recognition by Mapai (the ruling Labor party) of the significance of the professional contribution to a modern technological society was important because of its leadership role in society and government. Mapai believed that not only the state needed to harness the abilities of this group but the party also had to do this. According to Medding, Mapai leaders feared that without professionals, the party and the state would be left directionless and leaderless. In return for their services, Mapai could offer professionals the inducements and attractions of the party in power, dominant in the areas of decisionmaking relevant to their claims and interests.[90]

Israel's intelligentsia realized that the establishment of the state opened up opportunities to professionals, scientists, and scholars composing the new class. It also understood that the real power to make decisions was in the dominant Labor party. But here lay the seed of unease. The party elite was aware of the role of the new class in the life of the state but was unwilling to share power with it. The new class threatened the very foundations on which Labor's hegemony in Israeli society was based; professionals had to be co-opted without being strengthened politically. The Labor government thus refused to go along with wage demands of professionals, and the latter in turn refused to become an integral body of the Federation of Labor.[91] This reflected a deep conflict over political hegemony. As one party ideologue wrote, increase in the importance of science and learning in the life of modern society forced socialist movements to expand their base of support. No longer could the Labor party appeal only to the proletariat; it had to acknowledge the contribution of teachers, doctors, military men, engineers, scientists, and other professionals. But because these groups felt no solidarity with other workers, they were not given power—even though they were granted high status and were placed in high administrative positions.[92]

Whenever the party felt it might lose the vote of professionals or academics, it would hold urgent meetings to discuss the absorption of the "academic worker" or the "working intelligentsia" into the labor movement. A look at the minutes of these meetings, however, indicates the unwillingness of the party elite to integrate the new class into the circle of power. In April 1955, one week before elections to the council of the Federation of Labor and three months before the national elections, the party held a symposium as a result of its fear that it might lose the vote of professonals engaged in fierce wage struggles. The symposium was of great importance to the party; the prime minister and the minister of education and culture were present, and about 400 people were invited—writers and artists, scientists and researchers, doctors and engineers, educators, jurists, and others. The conference discussed "the role of the intellectual worker in the state and in the labor movement."[93]

The mention of both "state" and "movement" in the title had not been coincidental. The party's electoral support was based on its identification with the destiny of the state. In the past, this was made easy by the towering personality of Ben-Gurion. But gradually, new societal groups emerged that were not historically attached to the party and they advanced in the state administration. Applied scientists, for example, were almost exclusively associated with a small group of bureaucrats (known as "Ben-Gurion's boys") in the Ministry of Defense. These men were not treated as party loyalists, and the party thus made a great effort to co-opt the scientists.

Scientist Aharon Katchalski opened his lecture at the symposium by stating that science had become the rising economic force in the world. Machines had dominated economic change since the seventeenth century; in the twentieth century, science had become the leading force. He noted that developments in cybernetics, atomic energy, and other areas had transformed society and, consequently, the role of the traditional worker had been minimized. A new proletariat was rising, he said, composed of the better-educated people who could survive the process of automation. These people constituted a new sociological entity—a new proletariat—although they still possessed the consciousness of an intelligentsia.

The terms used by Katchalski were familiar to every party member in the audience. Like the old proletariat Karl Marx had in mind, the new proletariat was presented as being in control of the means of production, lacking only the consciousness necessary to assert that role. Katchalski explained that the problem was not how to recruit the new, technical intelligentsia—it had already been recruited. Thus, it posed a threat to the politician. This threat did not stem from the new proletariat's wage demands but from new ethical imperatives posed on society by science. For instance, Katchalski felt that science could not coexist with stale and frozen political frameworks. This point was raised in the ideological center of a party often accused of being stale and frozen. One can only imagine how party bosses felt when Katchalski added, a week before elections, that the new proletariat consisted of about 35,000 to 50,000 individuals. He concluded his lecture by claiming that all that was being done in the country was no longer the result of the adventurer but of the researcher.

The party elite was well aware of the threat posed by a new class that not only took credit for control of the means of production but demanded political power as well. Almost every professional speaking at that symposium, and at another one called to discuss the subject in July (closer to the national elections),[94] noted that the state-building process had not been conducted by bare-handed pioneers, as the party ideology claimed, but by engineers, agronomists, doctors, teachers, and lawyers. Professionals hinted that the growing importance of their professions entitled them to a greater say in national decisionmaking. The party leadership responded with contempt. "There is no need to mention the value of men of knowledge, those whose tools of work are what they have learned in the books in addition to their intellect," said Levi Eshkol, "but is the state dependent only on them? Tell me on whom the state is not dependent? If tomorrow the goat-milkers decide to go on strike, would the state not kneel before them?"[95]

Party leader Mordechai Namir claimed that Katchalski's analysis was actually consistent with traditional socialist doctrine. He admitted that the distinction between the worker and the intelligentsia would be blurred but insisted that this would happen as a result of increases in the educational level of the worker. Another party leader noted the need for the social education of the intellectuals, which would consist of an effort "to root them in the country, to wean them from any temptation, to harness them to the service of the whole, to plant in them the recognition they are workers of this state, pierced slaves of this state."[96]

The Labor party made several attempts to co-opt the new class. One attempt was the formation of a separate union for academic workers in the Federation of Labor. However, the conflict between the new class and the old guard was unbridgeable and the former became increasingly discontent. Indeed, in 1957 one party operative felt there was only one way left to "appease" the intelligentsia—have Ben-Gurion approach it as he had done successfully in the past.[97]

## The Scholars and Political Reform

The intelligentsia never really engaged in a struggle with the Labor party over hegemony of the state. I believe this realization by the intelligentsia contributed a great deal to its discontent in the 1960s.

Moreover, I believe that the intelligentsia's failure to assert its political power, or rather its potential political power, allows us to doubt whether it constituted a "class" in the fullest sense of the word. I will describe the dynamics involved by reference to one group—the scholars.

Israeli scholars had always been fascinated by Mapai's enormous power, which was unmatched by other political parties in the democratic world. The role of the party in shaping patterns of social life and in creating a Jewish state was widely acknowledged. The party's social-democratic ideology appealed to many scholars, as did its moderate and pragmatic style. Although some political scientists were critical of the party's dominance over the political system, most of them considered this dominance functional, a necessary prerequisite for a stable democracy.[98] It must also be recalled that scholars, like most Israelis, were brought in contact with the party in one stage or another of their lives—in the youth movement or kibbutz, for example—and developed sentimental, ideological, or personal ties to it. Thus, in spite of its increasing self-consciousness, the new class was not eager to engage in political conflict with the party elite, especially in light of the unprecedented control the party exercised on the state's finances, which included university budgets. This control may also partly explain the high participation rate of scholars at meetings held in the party's ideological center in Beit-Berl, which often surprised the organizers themselves. The list of participants in seminars held by the party reads like a "who's who" of Israeli scholarship, especially in the humanities and social sciences.

In 1961, a fierce succession struggle took place within the Labor party.[99] Pinhas Lavon, secretary-general of the Federation of Labor, demanded from Prime Minister Ben-Gurion a declaration of vindication concerning a security mishap that occurred six years earlier when Lavon was serving as minister of defense. Ben-Gurion's refusal turned into a struggle between the party's old guard, who supported Lavon, and the prime minister, backed by his young aides in the defense establishment (such as Moshe Dayan and Shimon Peres), whose rise to power terrified the party. In that struggle, the intelligentsia almost unanimously took the side of the party elite. Particularly effective was a public statement by Hebrew University professors, headed by the philosopher Nathan Rotenstreich, calling for the disassociation of the prime minister and the destiny of the state.[100] Lavon was presented as an individual seeking justice from the state leviathan, and the scholars fought for his case in Dreyfusian fashion.

During the Lavon affair, the scholars decided to form a political group within the party, devoted to the party's reform along the lines that guided their struggle for Lavon. They felt the time had come to rethink ideological issues and innovate the party accordingly. However, this group, calling itself *Min Hayessod* (from the foundation), soon realized this was impossible. Although the group sided with the party's old guard in regard to Lavon and a few other issues (the formation of the Labor Alignment, for example), the party hardly welcomed reformers. Less than a year after its formation, Min Hayessod called for blank ballots to be put in the ballot box at the 1961 elections as a sign of protest. In 1964 it split from the party altogether. Although there were many reasons for the split, it stemmed mainly from the realization that the Labor party did not allow for fresh thought along the lines cherished by the intellectual community in the 1960s. This was an era of belief in science, progressive education, ecologically conscious industrialization, apolitical public administration, national planning, and so on. These beliefs were taking hold in academia and the state bureaucracy but not in the Labor party.

This led to a fascinating paradox. Here was a new class that cherished values of modernization and innovation but was aligning, or rather trying to align, with the party elite—to whom these values constituted a threat. This was, of course, not so clear-cut. After all, many intellectuals could feel comfortable with the role they played in the transformation of power from Ben-Gurion to Eshkol, whose era as prime minister was marked by important societal changes. However, when facing a clear-cut choice in 1965, the intelligentsia chose power over innovation.

The need to choose came when Ben-Gurion and a handful of supporters split from the Labor party on the eve of the 1965 national elections and decided to run independently. The split was entirely the result of Ben-Gurion's personal caprice. This, by itself, was an advantage because the new party (named Rafi), in search of a program, was not obliged to hold to old clichés held by one or another party faction. Rafi's program was challenging to the intelligentsia because it committed the new party to everything the intelligentsia believed in.[101] For the first time in Israeli political life, nineteenth-century doctrines that guided all party programs were replaced by a call for a modern, innovative, technological state. Rafi demanded a change of the existing electoral system (based on proportional representation rather than on regional voting) as a means of weakening the control of political parties in the state, and called for modernization in agriculture, industry, education, social and economic policymaking, labor relations, and other areas. Although some of the terms used by Rafi sounded too technical even to the academic ear (especially the slogan "cybernation of the state"), the commitment to long-range planning, science, and innovation was in line with the preferences of the new class. Rafi spoke the intellectuals' language, derived its ideology from their books, and promised them an assertive role in the state.[102]

However, the intelligentsia did not join Rafi, nor did it support this party in the elections. This position did not stem from lack of understanding of the options involved. There was a clear choice between Rafi's "vigorous pragmatism" and "slogans generated decades earlier," wrote Leonard Fein.[103] And power seemed to be on the side of the latter. Rafi was a precariously organized new party with meager financial resources and no large pool of experienced personnel. Mapai, on the other hand, was a political giant, preeminently a symbol of stability.

In his discussion of the 1965 elections,[104] Eisenstadt noted that support of the Labor movement came largely from nonaligned groups—professional, academic, or industrial groups—who were far from accepting its socialist ideology. Why, then, did they vote for it? Eisenstadt's answer was that these groups voted either because of vested interests and some general feeling of well-being or because they were against the general overturning of the regime as advocated by Rafi. Whatever the answer may be, in 1965 the intelligentsia had clearly given up its role as a new class. Scholars did continue to talk about the need to innovate in Israeli society, and some even praised the Labor party's attempt to co-opt scientists and professionals as a response to Rafi's electoral challenge. But, as Eisenstadt noted, the party's ability to absorb new groups and to cater to their demands had always been greater than its ability to forge new orientations and policies.

There is no doubt that Eisenstadt knew the answer to the question he posed on the eve of the Six Day War: Would the institutional continuity of the Israeli political system, dependent entirely on the Mapai machine, "be connected with growing flexibility and innovation, or, conversely, with growing immobilization"?[105] It was the intelligentsia's realization that it had voted against innovation and for immobilization that explains its response to the 1967 crisis. As the crisis started, members of the intelligentsia were among the first to express fear that the country was ruled by Labor party politicians. When faced with real danger, they called for the nomination of Rafi's Moshe Dayan as minister of defense.

# Chapter Four

# The Challenge of War

One of the characteristics of Jewish literary culture is the lack of war songs. In order to find this genre in Jewish culture, one must go back to the Old Testament. When the ark went forward, Moses said: "Rise up, O Lord, and let Thine enemies be scattered" (Numbers 10:35). In the song of the prophet Deborah we find some of the typical boasting of the warrior in the ancient world: "Then did the horsehooves stamp by reason of the prancings, the prancings of their mighty ones" (Judges 5:22). Most war songs were composed by the prophets, such as Jeremiah, in times of danger, but even these remained insignificant compared to the prophets' visions of peace. Jewish holidays memorialize many historical events, but very few of them concern war and victory. At Hanukka, the heroism of the Maccabees is praised, but it is their spiritual resistance to religious persecution that is emphasized. A Jewish proverb considers heroes as those who control their passions. On Passover, the Jewish people thank the Lord for liberating them from slavery instead of thanking him for the conquest of Canaan.

In the nineteenth century, when national movements revived the sagas of ancient war heroes, the Jewish writer was in trouble. Lacking a tradition of warfare, there was little material to rely on, and most writers had to resort to the epics of Bar-Kokhba, who launched a rebellion against the Roman Empire in the second century A.D. Although the rebellion ended in total disaster, poets such as Yehuda L. Gordon, Naphtali H. Imber, Yaacov Cohen, and Hayim N. Bialik revived the legends concerning Bar-Kokhba, especially one about his victory in the gladiator's ring over a lion.[1] Most epics used biblical materials, such as the victories of the judges Samson and Gideon or David's fight with Goliath. Sometimes, the epics had to be borrowed from other cultures, as were Zalman Schneour's epics of Spartacus, the slave-rebel whose revenge is yet to be taken by all oppressed people.[2]

It is interesting that of all the epics developed by the Jewish national movement, the only one that remained part of the symbol system in

Israel after independence was that of Massada.[3] Massada is a mountain in the Judean desert to which Jewish rebels and their families escaped after the rebellion against Rome in A.D. 70. They survived a three-year-long Roman siege and finally committed suicide in order not to be taken alive. The epos of Massada, revived by the poet Yitzhak Lamdan, is one of persistence and ingenuity, not one of victory. So are the poems written during the War of Independence. The poems associated with that war—"Bab El-Waad" by Haim Gouri, "Shayara Shelanu" by Nathan Yonathan, or "Hayu Zemanim" by Hayyim Hefer—are all characterized by sensitivity to the tragedy of war and hope for another day when "cyclamens will bloom."[4]

In the 1960s, when Israel's intellectuals took on the role of social critics, they naturally raised many questions about war and peace. Is Israel doing enough to pursue peace with its Arab neighbors? To what degree does it have control over peace in the Middle East? How well does it treat its Arab citizens? What should be the model of Israeli-Arab relations in the long run? To what degree should Israel strive for cultural integration in the region? Meetings were held, associations were founded, and journals, devoted to these questions, such as *New Outlook*, were published.

Some of the most important literary works of the 1960s were reflections on the Arab-Israeli conflict and the question of peace. A. B. Yehoshua's *Facing the Forests* became the most-discussed short story of the era.[5] It describes a student guarding a forest planted on the ruins of an Arab village and cooperating with an old Arab who puts it on fire. This surrealistic tale had hard political implications, but the book-reading community was willing to pick up the challenge. The tale was treated as a societal contribution because it added an important dimension to the public dialogue in Israel. By courageously exposing a moral double standard, wrote Amos Elon in *The Israelis*,[6] Yehoshua may be considered a better citizen than all self-righteous patriots.

One wonders how long a society can maintain such a high appreciation for self-reflection under the challenge of war. Since Yehoshua published this short story, four wars were fought in the Middle East that had an impact on the intellectual dialogue. In this chapter, I would like to demonstrate the challenge in reference to the Six Day War of 1967 when the intellectual community, in a moment of great fear, abandoned critical discourse and resorted to messianic thinking. I will show how the messianic tendencies of the intellectuals, only partly curbed by the short experience of statehood, overwhelmed their perception of reality when they were faced with the danger of annihilation. I shall also discuss the messianic interpretation of the victory and explain it as a closing of the gap described in the former chapter between vision and reality. In 1967, reality no longer seemed petty, and the intellectuals were redeemed. First, however, I would like to put the intellectuals' response to the war in theoretical perspective. It would be wrong to perceive it as unique. Elsewhere, intellectuals have shown a similar tendency to replace, during war, critical discourse with ideological slogans, political messianism, or sheer silence.

## War and the Intellectuals

"When war is declared we all go mad," said George Bernard Shaw, referring to the enthusiastic response of his fellow intellectuals to the outbreak of World War I.[7] This seems to be a recurrent phenomenon. When war breaks out, intellectuals often turn away from the careful, self-reflective discourse for which they are known, feeling that at time of war the sword must be given primacy over the pen. The scholarly literature found that this feeling resulted in behavior such as the embracing of military service,[8] engaging in propaganda and other activities that subordinate intellectual work to the national interest,[9] self-imposition of restrictions on academic freedom,[10] and the replacing of elaborate speech variants by simple, emotional, patriotic rhetoric.[11] As Randolph Bourne observed, "Once the war is on, the conviction  spreads that individual thought is helpless, that the only way one can count is as a cog in the great wheel."[12]

When war is over, intellectuals are the first to lament the lack of self-reflection when it was perhaps most needed. A condition of war involves important deliberations: What constitutes a casus belli? Is war inevitable? What nature should it take? How far should it be carried out? What restraints ought to be self-imposed, and which could be abandoned? How should victory or defeat be interpreted? In retrospect it is always agreed that these questions should not be left to politicians and generals alone: The intellectual's universalist perspective—one transcending the prevailing social sentiment at any given time— is as necessary in war as in peace. But during war, the intellectual prefers to remain silent, leaving the deliberations to those in charge and frequently turning against intellectual discourse itself. "We valued ourselves as cool calculators," wrote Ralph Waldo Emerson during the American Civil War; "we were fine with our learning and culture, with our science that was of no country and our religion of peace—and now a sentiment mightier than logic, wide as light, strong as gravity, reaches into the college, the bank, the farm-house, and the church."[13]

Emerson was, indeed, one of the greatest American thinkers in the nineteenth century, a self-conscious intellectual, cherishing, in *The American Scholar,* the privacy and detachment of the intellectual from institutions. He was known for saying that "good men must not obey the laws too well." Just a few days before the South's attack on Fort Sumter in 1861, Emerson was willing to see the Union and its institutions go to pieces for the sake of individualism. And yet, as reported in George Frederickson's study on Northern intellectuals and the crisis of the Union, Emerson rejoiced over the patriotic response of the masses after the attack, as did Walt Whitman, who had previously put forth a noninstitutional creed for the United States. In his "Beat! Beat! Drums!" Whitman rejoiced in the manner of Emerson at the way the war spirit went into the school where the scholar was studying.

The more straightforward the intellectual's universalism, the more puzzling such embracing of the war seems to others and to the intellectual when it is over. A case in point is H. G. Wells, who abhorred any form of nationalism that "trumpets and waves its flags, obtrudes its tawdry loyalties, exaggerates the splendours of its past, and fights to sustain the ancient hallucinations."[14] Nationalism was considered by Wells the antithesis to intellect because it subverts the intellect and prevents a rational discourse of scientific facts. To Wells, political and social institutions should be based on scientific and technological principles that are, by their nature, cosmopolitan. And yet the same writer found himself overwhelmed by the outbreak of World War I. "The world disaster, now that it had come, so overwhelmed my mind that I was obliged to thrust a false interpretation upon it, and assert, in spite of my deep and at first unformulated misgivings, that here and now, the new world order was in conflict with the old."[15]

How did such a shift in Wells's worldview come about? Edward Mead Earle, who studied this question, found the answer in the words of one of Wells's heroes, William Clissold II: "My intellect is cosmopolitan but my pride and instincts are patriotic."[16] Wells, wrote Earle, believed in the transformation of the national state into a universal one, but he was also an English patriot. And the English patriot, as George Bernard Shaw noted, "not only lost his head but insisted on kicking it around the streets as well."[17]

The tendency of intellectuals in World War I to silence critical discourse and yield their universalist perspective to crude patriotism was widespread in all the belligerent countries. As Randolph Bourne, a famous objector to U.S. intervention in the war, wrote in 1917, the war "reduced to rubbish" most of the humanitarian internationalism and democratic nationalism that had been the emotional thread of the American intellectual. "We go to war to save the world from subjugation! But the German intellectuals went to war to save their culture from barbarization! And the French went to war to save their beautiful France! And the English to save international honor! And Russia, most altruistic and self-sacrificing of all, to save a small State from destruction! Whence is our miraculous intuition of our moral spotlessness?"[18]

Bourne accused his fellow intellectuals in the United States of solving the moral dilemmas involved in support of the war not by the "higher synthesis" expected of them but by a reversion to primitive ways of thinking: "Simple syllogisms are substituted for analysis, things are known by their labels, our heart's desire dictates what we shall see."[19] Failing to synthesize conflicting values, intellectuals regressed to ideas that could be realized in quick, simplified action. Thought became any easy rationalization of what was actually going on or what is inevitably going to happen tomorrow.

Bourne noticed that U.S. intellectuals were troubled about going to war. Whereas European intellectuals had only to rationalize and justify what their countries were already doing, the intellectuals of the neutral United States were burdened with the search for truth. This is why they were greatly relieved when neutrality ended: "At last action, irresponsibility, the end to anxious and torturing attempts to reconcile peace-ideals with the drag of the world towards Hell."[20] The hesitations, ironies, consciences, and considerations of the intellectual were drowned in the elemental blare of doing something aggressive and colossal. Bourne, in a strong and vivid comment on the intellectual's turning idealogue, talked about a "peacefulness of being at war," a "thankfulness" for the opportunity to lay down the hesitation and suspense. "The American university," he reported, "is a brisk and happy place these days. Simple, unquestioning action had suspended the knots of thought. The thinker dances with reality."[21]

Historians were puzzled by intellectuals' tendency to release themselves of the burden of intellect once war began. The silence of the intellectuals was intriguing when in World War I a flourishing European intellectual community—supposedly devoted to cosmopolitianism, not to mention those devoted to socialist internationalism— turned patriotic overnight. And the causes were generally attributed to the intellectuals themselves rather than to constraints posed on them. Two studies, one by a sociologist and one by a historian of ideas, are particularly useful in defining the phenomenon and pointing to its explanation.

The first is Carol Gruber's book *Mars and Minerva*,[22] dealing with the response of the U.S. academic community to the challenge of World War I. She was concerned mainly with the American academic community's conception that the war made special demands on the man of knowledge. As one historian expressed it: "This is one of the times when I feel that the pen is not mightier than the sword."[23] The author's main thesis is that the manner in which U.S. professors embraced the war and war service may be viewed in part as an expression of uncertainty about their social status and role. After searching the archives of institutions of higher learning, she came to the conclusion that there was a strain of professional insecurity behind the intellectuals' positive commitment to be of service during a time of national crisis, often to the extent of betraying their role as intellectuals (for example, historians engaging in the type of propaganda that amounts to mental corruption).

Gruber felt that a sense of uncertainty over the role of the university, the purpose and value of the academic profession, and belonging in the larger social world was shown in the professors' desire to leap into the service as fighting soldiers or even as manual workers. The academics' uncertainty was shown in the desire to enter surrogate service by those who were left behind. The quest for purpose and "reality" outside campus walls suggested to her a view of the university and academic profession as unreal and lacking in purpose. She considered the professors' response to war as an attempted escape from alienation. Lacking a conviction in the value of their work, professors sought to establish their own values by participating in the world of affairs. Lacking a sense of community among their peers, professors sought it in war service.

In a study entitled *Redemption by War,*[24] Ronald Stromberg told how on August 3, 1914, Bertrand Russell had no trouble collecting signatures on an antiwar manifesto, but the next day all the signers changed their minds. As the guns of August began to roar, the conventional antiwar rhetoric gave way to an intellectual spirit that conceived the war all over Europe as one of renewal, adventure, and apocalypse. Although the author admitted that intellectuals had little to do with the beginning of the war, which was sparked by statesmen who were largely immersed in their own world, he claimed that the intellectuals' approbation contributed to the war's endurance and to such policies as annexationism, "war to the utmost," and the refusal of peace terms. Intellectuals staffed the propaganda ministries, wrote the books and articles of what became the most literary of wars, and created the war's extravagant mystique. A mysticism of violence, wrote Stromberg, flickered behind the August guns, and the tragedy was tempered by the abundant assurance from sages and savants that the war would bring about a resurrection, a purification, a liberation.

Stromberg searched for the causes of the war spirit among the intellectuals in the intellectual history of Europe on the eve of the war. He explained it by their hatred of the existing society, an apocalyptic sense of an ending, the need for some kind of worthy cause to give meaning to one's life, a sheer thirst for adventure against the background of a dreary materialism, the belief that somehow burning away the old would prepare for a clean, new order of things and—above all—a desire to rejoin the national community in order to repair the divisions of a fragmented, sundered society.

Europe's intellectuals shared a vision of social harmony and solidarity, a curing of alienation and isolation, and of a society marked by a distributive justice and by fulfillment for each unique individual within a harmonious whole. Such a vision seems to grow especially among intellectuals who sense fragmentation and loss of social solidarity as a result of excessive intellectualizing and analyzing. The intellectual, as person of the word who transcends communal conventions and deals with universal norms, may easily fall into the mood, identified by Stromberg in fin de siècle Europe, whereby the word "lost its felt identity with reality, became separated from the object, was seen to be an abstraction totally divorced from the world."[25]

One should not draw false analogies from the experience of World War I. Like every historical event, it was in most ways unique, and the intellectuals' response to the war was affected by specific notions prevailing at the time—such as the Bergsonian revolt of the soul against reason or the Darwinian survival of the fittest. Also the shift from universalism to parochialism in World War I was particularly stunning. At the same time, the explanations offered for the intellectuals' response, which related it to their own identity qua intellectuals, seem to apply generally. The intellectuals' special position vis-à-vis the community (likened by Dahrendorf to that of the Shakespearean fool[26]), and their subsequent difficulty in living with their trade, is common enough to consider it a predicting variable of intellectuals' political behavior in varying circumstances.

It is hard to explain the intellectuals' silencing of their discourse during war, whatever form the silencing took, merely by the circumstances of that war. Even when their behavior seems "understandable" in light of the circumstances, as many would argue in regard to the Six Day War, it amounts to the willingness of an important social elite to abandon its social role, a phenomenon whose explanation—as the experience of World War I leads us to believe—must be sought in the political sociology of the intellectual.

However understandable the silence of the intellectuals in the Six Day War was in light of the circumstances, its sources lie in the difficult encounter between the intellectual and the state. An explanation that relies merely on the circumstances of the war and does not consider this encounter can hardly account for the special nature of the intellectuals' response, that is, their tendency to abandon the independent and deliberate word. One must recall that this happened in a society that cherished the spoken and written word. Thus, there is good reason to believe that the intellectuals' behavior was motivated by deep disquiet.

*[handwritten margin notes: casus belli; an act justifying war; a reason for war]*

I will now describe this behavior and its far-reaching political implications.

## The Intellectuals' Response to the Threat

On May 15, 1967, a vast Egyptian military force moved into the Sinai desert, the buffer zone between Egypt and Israel. This move was made at a time of continuous tension on the border between Israel and Egypt's ally—Syria. A month earlier, in April, that tension had reached a high point when the Syrians mined main roads in northern Israel and shelled settlements, and the Israelis on April 7 took a reprisal action in which seven Syrian planes were downed. Alarmed by Israeli planes flying over Syria's capital, Damascus, on that occasion, the Soviet Union played an active role in persuading Gamal Abdel Nasser to take a deterring step against Israel and to show solidarity with his Syrian allies.

The crisis escalated on May 16 when Nasser demanded the evacuation of United Nations forces that served as a buffer between Egypt and Israel, and U Thant, the UN general secretary, zealously agreed. As the evacuation took place, Israel, surrounded by numerically superior forces, began to appeal to world governments for help. The futility of the appeal became clear as the days went by and especially after Nasser, on May 22, closed the Straits of Tiran to Israeli shipping, a move that constituted a casus belli in the Middle East. The whole world stood by, holding its breath, while Israeli diplomats made pathetic attempts to convince world governments to honor their previous commitments to the freedom of navigation.

In Israel, fear mounted to unprecedented heights, nourished by an intense propaganda campaign in the neighboring countries, by memories of the Holocaust, when the world also stood by as Jews faced extermination, and by one traumatic incident. On May 28, in the midst of the crisis, Levi Eshkol, Israel's prime minister and minister of defense, known to be a weak leader, made a speech to deter the enemy and calm the nation but managed to get his notes mixed up and ended up with an embarrassing stuttering on the radio. On June 2, partly as a result of that incident, a national unity government was established, and Eshkol was forced to yield the defense portfolio to Moshe Dayan, hero of the 1956 Sinai War. This change opened the way to a preemptive strike launched by Israel on June 5 against Egypt, Syria, and Jordan, which resulted in victory within six days.[27]

As tension mounted on the borders, Moshe Dor, a young poet associated with the Israeli Left, published an article in which he expressed many intellectuals' feelings. Overnight, poetry had become

5-23-91

"pale" in his eyes. The individual poet seemed "tragically arrogant" to him all of a sudden and the collective experience was overwhelming.[28] This was an explicit statement, in the Israeli context, of a common feeling of intellectuals that their trade was superfluous and their individualism wrong in moments of national crisis. Consider the following expression by another young poet, Louis MacNeice, during the Spanish Civil War: "As soon as I heard on the wireless of the outbreak of war, Galway became unreal. And Yeats and his poetry became unreal also. This was not merely because Galway and Yeats belong in a sense to a past order of things. The unreality which now overtook them was also overtaking in my mind modern London, modernist art, and Left Wing politics."[29]

Although the situations in which the two poets found themselves were very different, their responses were not. Poetry was dismissed during the crisis not because it disturbed the war effort—only few poets believe poetry has such an influence—but because it belonged to a different "reality." It is not merely intellectuals' tools that become superfluous but also their world—one cherishing individualism, universalism, modernism, and left-wing politics. In his article, Moshe Dor came close to demanding of the intellectual to be quiet altogether: "Perhaps we are all destined to keep quiet now, in the sense that the private idiosyncracies must be silent as long as the scales are moving on which the nation's fate is weighed. When things get better, they will be allowed to speak. Now, only he should speak in whose voices are reflected the voices of his brothers."[30] Other intellectuals concurred. During the crisis, seven writers were approached by the literary supplement of one newspaper for their comment on the role of the artist in times of national emergency. Of the seven men, five refused to be interviewed, claiming, according to the editor, that "the artist has no role in these days, he is simply superfluous." Of the two who did comment, one was quoted as saying that "the only contribution the artist can make at this time is to sign up for reserve duty."[31]

The silence of the intellectuals was often more subtle but no less significant. I refer to those instances in which intellectuals did not refrain from political comment but instead adjusted their statements to the new situation. This took various forms. Some intellectuals confined their statements to those adhering to the public sentiment, or they justified the public sentiment by associating it with universal norms. Other intellectuals redefined formerly held universal norms in a way that facilitated political rationalization, or they simply declared the universal to be inferior to the parochial. These terms are not absolute, of course. What constitutes a universal norm is itself socially and culturally determined. The abandonment of a universalist perspective depends on the way it was previously perceived and on the degree to which it was distinguished from parochial interests in the first place. In the case we deal with here, however, the distinctions were very clear.

As we saw, on the eve of the Six Day War, Israel's intellectuals perpetuated well-known norms of the Western world. They had played a major role in the transformation of Israel in the 1960s from a mobilized society engaged in nation building to a liberal democracy. With the Western world uncooperative once again toward Jews threatened with annihilation, these norms were the first to be questioned in light of current affairs. Poet Nathan Zach was quite clear on this point when, on June 30, he commented that the Kantian principle of eternal peace had now been put second to the principle of evil revealed by recent history.[32] It is not surprising that Israeli intellectuals in 1967 would draw gloomy lessons from history—the situation very much resembled familiar scenes in Jewish history. Even a routine announcement by the civil defense authorities instructing citizens how to behave during bombings could raise traumatic memories: "When at home; fall down, crawl under an object; in the street: fall down, defend your neck and ears with your hand. . . . When you go to sleep in your flat: prepare at your bed a morning gown, a darkened hand-lamp and your clothes. If you have small children—prepare the necessary things for them (clothing, blankets, food) in a well-packed bundle."[33]

Two decades after the Holocaust, it was again necessary for Israeli Jews to sleep with packed bundles at their sides—the symbol of the wandering Jew in history. Having escaped the ghetto, never to return, they looked for shelter under something as their ancestors did during pogroms. Individuals in a modern, cosmopolitan society were to fall down and cover their neck and ears with their hands. No wonder the intellectuals, particularly aware of such symbolism, could not continue to view the world from the perspective of their peers in other, safer, liberal democracies. As one writer declared on May 31 when the sense of danger and frustration was at a peak, the whole of Jewish civilization was at stake, and this called for a new voice to be sounded loud and clear in the country—louder than all the voices of battle since the ancient Maccabeans and the heroes of Massada.[34]

The intellectuals temporarily placed Kantian principles and other universalist norms second to imperatives derived from Jewish history and myth. The abstract principle of world peace had to yield to the demands of the day. This does not imply its abandonment; it does imply a high probability of giving up in the long run that special, additional sensitivity one develops when considering history in light of Kantian imperatives.

It seems as if some nations have the privilege of pursuing universalist notions while others, challenged by war, are doomed to view the world from a parochial perspective. Consider the following incident that occurred on May 15, Israel's Independence Day, just one day before the beginning of the 1967 crisis. An Independence Day ceremony took place in Jerusalem in which a poem by the prominent poet Nathan Alterman was to be read. The poem mentioned the thin line dividing the blessing of peace and the curse of war. A university professor who heard the poem during a rehearsal found it too chauvinistic and, together with others, pressured the prime minister's office not to allow the poem to be read. The event triggered high-level consultations in the prime minister's office until finally a compromise was found. A special envoy was sent to the poet, who asked him to change the words "a thin line divides" to "consider the difference" in the poem written eleven years earlier. "This is how Alterman saved the country," one newspaper reported, mocking the blown-up incident.[35] It was blown up, but it was also indicative of the enormous sensitivity to the norm of peace, conceived not only as a political concept reflecting real or declaratory interests but also as a cultural imperative. Before the Six Day War, both language and peace were important: Public language was not allowed to resemble the boasting of warriors.

In no society do such delicacies win intellectuals much popularity. They are known everywhere as "peaceniks." It is thus not surprising that during the 1967 crisis, when a strong government was called for, intellectuals were referred to by nonintellectuals as a conscientious elite "of whose type the surrender governments of Czechoslovakia, Norway, etc. were composed."[36] However, a close look at the intellectuals' behavior during the crisis reveals this stereotype to be wrong: Intellectuals played a leading role in the public outcry for an emergency government. This was notable for three reasons. First, the Israeli intelligentsia had, as a general rule, previously supported Prime Minister Eshkol, whose open, democratic style was in line with its preferences. Many intellectuals had played an active role in the political process in the early 1960s that brought Eshkol to power as an alternative to Prime Minister Ben-Gurion, whom they considered authoritarian. In their comments about an emergency government, one can find a clear confession of guilt over that role. One political scientist, for instance, called for a return of Ben-Gurion to the scene,[37] in spite of the fact that Ben-Gurion was eighty-one years old at the time and quite exhausted by the political struggles over the Lavon affair.

Second, the intellectuals' call for an emergency government included a dismissal of "politics as usual" and the search for a savior to transcend that process. This is significant because Israel's intellectuals were all too aware that politics is, as Bernard Crick put it, "a test of freedom."[38] Israel's intellectuals cherished democracy, played an active part in the formation of the country's constitutional setup, and engaged in pressure-group politics. Now they were involved in the search for what one critic called "mythological figures"[39] who would avoid the wheeling and dealing of politics and lead the nation to victory.

For instance, on May 26 one writer contended that the military must be confident that behind it stands a leadership "destined" to the task instead of "a puzzle of political parties."[40] On May 28, when Golda Meir, secretary-general of the incumbent Labor party, objected to a national unity government, another writer warned that "in all due respect to the services of Mrs. Meir and similar party leaders, there is no doubt we can win every war without the active help of Labor's secretariat."[41] On the same day, one columnist who was also searching for "a person or persons who could lead us" reminded his readers that "we have no labor dispute with Nasser and the debate with him is not over the adjustment of salaries to the cost of living."[42] On June 2, seven professors of political science signed a petition calling for "national leadership," explaining its benefits in professional terms.[43] When on that day a national unity government was formed, and Moshe Dayan was nominated minister of defense, writer Yeshurun Keshet felt he no longer had to think. "From now on, the Minister of Defense has the answers," said an entry in his diary.[44]

Third, the intellectuals' support of Dayan required their giving up many previously held norms. This point had been overlooked in later accounts of the Six Day War, most of which considered it "natural" that the wheel of state in a democratic society facing crisis be given to an ex-general. Randolph and Winston Churchill, for instance, wrote: "In the face of the crisis the Israeli people turned to one man— General Moshe Dayan, the victor of Sinai in 1956. Here was a man who had the knowledge and ability to assess the situation and make a decision."[45]

It is still hard to determine whether Dayan's appointment was truly needed in the 1967 crisis or whether the decision to launch a preemptive strike, made before his naming, could have been carried out with equal success without the transfer of power. What is clear is that Dayan played a symbolic role and answered largely irrational needs. As analyzed by Walter Laqueur in *The Road to War,* the movement for a national unity government was partly the result of a sincere belief that in the hour of crisis all party differences should be forgotten, and partly the result of a sudden wave of emotion, which, though short of panic or mass hysteria, was "certainly deeply irrational, reflecting an almost mystical belief that the 'victor of Sinai' could save Israel."[46] Regarding it from the perspective of the intelligentsia, this was irrational indeed because Dayan represented everything it detested—opportunism, unpredictability, and a measure of lawlessness.

One of Dayan's biographers wondered who he really was: "Is he really the prototype of the leader for an embattled nation, leaping to the forefront and rallying the entire nation with the inflaming cry: After me! Or is he, perhaps, nothing more than a dangerous adventurer, exciting the blind mass with personal publicity tactics and occasionally vaulting into the saddle of leadership without being able to retain his hold and to prove the permanency of his success?"[47] The intelligentsia was aware of the second set of qualities mentioned in this quotation but had put them aside. Neither did it give consideration to the costs his nomination might incur. To the contrary—Dayan's symbolic image as savior had now been nourished exactly by those characteristics that were most criticized before—his disregard for law and procedure, his solitary style of operation, his impatience with detail, his bold and often irresponsible encounters with danger, perhaps even his reputation as womanizer. Dayan was needed at the wheel of state, claimed the Churchills, because of his "knowledge, courage and optimism."[48] Sharing in the public quest for a savior, the intelligentsia did not stop to ask whether the ex-general was really more knowledgeable than the prime minister, more courageous than the chief of staff, or more optimistic than any other politician.

## Victory and Messianism

It would be wrong to level the charge of "betrayal" against the intellectuals for their behavior during the three weeks of the 1967 crisis. Their response to the crisis was largely affected by their fear, which their intellect could not diminish. Intellectuals can be expected to cast doubt on established notions, such as the necessity of preemptive strike or the notion of Dayan as savior. But as cool thinkers, they cannot be expected to be at their best when surprised by a military force launching a wild propaganda campaign devoted to their destruction. It is even understandable that people facing such conditions would give up their thinking altogether and find refuge in the community. However, this behavior becomes questionable when it continues after the danger is over. Many aspects of the intellectuals' behavior took on a different meaning after the victory: their silence, their willingness to give up universalist thinking, their adherence to the "lessons of history," their support of mythological figures, and their abandonment of reality for the sake of myth.

One of the intellectuals' responses to the stunning victory in the Six Day War was to abandon the independent and deliberate word. Few empirical, analytical, or critical statements about reality were heard; intellectuals were using an unusual number of metaphors denying the temporal and spatial dimensions of reality. The victory was described as a "miracle," the occupied lands were described as "holy," and the soldiers became those who fulfilled a transhistorical mission. The most common expression after the victory was the biblical verse "We were like unto them that dream" (Psalms 126:1). Biblical verses seemed more appropriate to describe the new, transcendental reality than common language seemed. One intellectual, for instance, expressed his desire to scream publicly: "Arise O Lord, and let thy enemies be scattered" (Numbers 10:35).

The abandonment of the temporal and spatial dimensions of reality in the face of victory is common in human history. Since time immemorial, victory has sparked transcendental feelings, and modernity has not diminished the role of the writer who transcends the blood and tears of war (or the difficulties of coping with the postwar situation) and sings praises to the Lord. It is also common to find changes in rhetoric resulting from the feeling that one is participating in a mighty historical drama.[49]

For example, describing his entry into Rome with the U.S. army in World War II, Glenn Gray wrote that "the Eternal City was welcoming another conqueror. . . . I felt like one of the soldiers who took the city thousands of years before."[50] By turning into an "eternal city," Rome of June 1944 ceased to be simply a troubled, conquered city: A bridge was built over the generations and the city became myth. Intellectuals, especially writers and poets, are known to play a major role in the creation and dissemination of myths as part of their "unusual sensitivity to the sacred."[51] This was particularly interesting in light of the Israeli intelligentsia and its ambivalence toward the messianic tradition.

The intellectual's inspiration is often found in the meeting point between the earthly and the spiritual.[52] In Jewish scholarly tradition, however, the intellectual could not be endowed with such messianic powers because of the interdiction, "For man shall not look at me and live" (Exodus 33:20). As we have seen before, the word was viewed more often as a concealment than as a revealment of the transcendental. Thus, whenever the urge developed to give up the written or spoken word, the Jewish intellectual became uncomfortable. People were not expected to cross the fences between the earthly and transcendental dimensions of reality, or between themselves and the world concealed by the word. To a large extent, Jewish intellectual history was the history of the struggle—often a struggle in the intellectual's own mind—between the scholarly and messianic traditions.[53]

But in 1967 the Israeli intelligentsia turned messianic. The earthly and the spiritual merged and the intellectual was absorbed in that majestic experience to the extent of giving up the word altogether. Writer Moshe Shamir was explicit. Words, he was reported to have said in a public lecture, are a means to discipline symbols and to deliver them wrapped up and nicely dressed. But of what use are words when the symbols are walking among us on the streets? Of what use are talking and thinking when unimaginative things happen that are more real than reality?[54]

The feeling was that reality itself was the stuff dreams were made of. As another writer put it on the same day, the chattering of idlers on street corners had become history and the gossip of women knitting socks had become the biography of a nation.[55] In those days, events occurring in real time were described as occurring in no time, and geographical locations were described as mythological scenes. Writer Aharon Megged joined the forces that conquered the Temple Mount; here is his report: "Where are we located in the calendar? The return to Zion? The days of Zerubbabel? The days of Bilu?—A great past, the annals of a peoples, are suddenly standing still for one moment, one tear."[56]

Zerubbabel was the first to return from the Babylonian exile in the sixth century B.C., and Bilu was the first group of Zionist immigrants from Russia who settled in Palestine in 1882. This statement blurs the temporal dimension and ties the conquest of the Temple Mount with all the returns to Zion. By doing so, it endows the conquest of 1967 (and for that matter the immigration of 1882) with the holiness previously reserved for the original Temple Mount. Megged, a secular writer, associated—unintentionally perhaps—the military and political reality of 1967 with biblical mythology such as the following: "And the Lord stirred up the spirit of Zerubbabel the son of Shealtiel, governor of Judah, and the spirit of Joshua the son of Jehozadak, the high priest, and the spirit of all the remnant of the people; and they came and did work in the house of the Lord of hosts, their God" (Haggai 1:14).

The blurring of the temporal dimension was accompanied by disregard for the spatial one. In the first reports from the war, the fact was sometimes ignored that the occupied territories in the West Bank were real geographical entities inhabited by close to a million Arabs. In Megged's report, there was only the Holy Land: "This is the holy-land, the land of the forefathers. . . . Not far from the present Arab city of Jenin, Joseph and his brothers drove their cattle, not far from Ramallah,

Jacob saw the ladder in his dream. Anathoth is the birthplace of Jeremiah, Samaria was a kingdom's capital."[57]

This messianic approach may have set the intellectual background for policies that ignored empirical reality for the sake of illusions. In 1967, Israel found itself in control of territories that were three times its original size. Instead of engaging in deep analysis, its intelligentsia perpetuated ancient biblical myths. Several years later they flocked to the peace movements and asked how religious motives came to affect Israeli foreign policy after 1967. The answer, I believe, may be partly found in the behavior of the secular intelligentsia. Its incumbents—hawks and doves alike—were willing to ask, like Megged, "Where are we located in the calendar?" and accept as an answer that all of Jewish history stood still on June 5–10, 1967. The tanks and half-tracks that won a modern war became the Messiah's messengers.

I also think that the intelligentsia's impact on the public, which conceived the victory in messianic rather than empirical terms, may have been greater than generally believed due to a unique sociological reason: Writers are usually more prone than others to messianic dreams. In the 1967 war, many writers were recruited as military correspondents; therefore the news about victories in the various fronts was transmitted to the Israeli public wrapped in messianic interpretation. No wonder the general public, hearing about the conquest of the Western Wall as a moment in which all of Jewish history stood still, came to consider the six days of the war as the six days of Creation. The conquest of the Temple Mount was seen as a return to "the Temple." It was like a moment in which 2,000 years of history had disappeared—a meeting between the paratroopers who arrived there in 1967 and the Jews who defended it during Roman times. Accompanying the fighting troops who reached the Temple Mount was the chief army rabbi, blowing the shofar. As every intellectual with a historical perspective must have known, this insensitive act—carrying out a religious ritual in a place holy to three religions—could threaten Jewish–Moslem relations for generations. Yet only one intellectual publicly objected to "the clown with the horn."[58] Others felt, as Moshe Dor admitted, that the artist's intuition does not have the power to compete with the shofar.[59] The intelligentsia, joining in the community's euphoria, had literally given up the word and with it, the perspective of those who evaluate the world from a certain distance.

The difficulty in distancing oneself from the events and considering them historical rather than transhistorical is well illustrated in the statement by one writer, Shulamith Hareven,[60] who associated her own identity with that of the city of Jerusalem as described in Psalms. When Jerusalem was reunited in 1967, she felt she had gained back her lost identity "as a city that is compact together" (Psalms 122:3). The same writer defined the situation in the Middle East by an analogy to a dolphin attacked by an eagle. The source of that analogy is a discussion of war between civilization and barbarism in *The New Leviathan* by Oxford's R. G. Collingwood.[61] "We may close the book and let Oxford know: the dolphin has won,"[62] she wrote on June 9. What is instructive here is not the analogy itself but the idea of the closing of the book, proposed by an intellectual in light of a new truth revealed by crude reality.

Paradoxically, the refusal to consider reality in its concrete dimensions did not prevent some intellectuals from deriving lessons from it. Although history turned into mythology, it still taught them a lesson—one that stood in contrast to previously held universalist norms. An interesting example can be found in an article by Shabtai Tevet, a journalist and biographer, the title of which may be translated as: "The Good Ones to the Air Force!"[63] That slogan, used by the army in its recruitment efforts, raised a philosophical debate in the early 1960s. Intellectuals objected to the association of the universal value of "good" with an earthly institution like the air force. "The good ones to good deeds," the philosopher Nathan Rotenstreich proposed as an alternative, "and the pilots to the air force!"[64] On June 20, 1967, after the air force's great success in the war, Tevet published the article that demanded that the intellectuals who had previously objected to the slogan "go down on their knees and ask for forgiveness." In Tevet's view, scholars who had considered the slogan inappropriate were proven wrong by the circumstances. The luxury of being an intellectual who closes his eyes to the facts, he added, is no longer an option for an Israeli. Whether or not the slogan is sound, he added, is determined not by anybody's will or policy but by the tough reality.

This was the major consequence of the war from the point of view of the intellectuals: "Reality" would now prevail over intellect. But reality itself had been transcended and conceived in messianic terms. A new "realism" thus came into being: Intellectuals took their own messianic illusions as real and dismissed empirical observation as a source of insights about the environment. They were overwhelmed by the lessons "history" had taught the nation, for example, that the status of the Jew as pariah in the world had not changed with the establishment of the state of Israel. At the same time, they ignored lessons from history, that is, that whatever one's status in the world, whether pariah or not, it is worthwhile to take the initiative in foreign affairs rather than stay idle—as Dayan's Israel tended to do.

By learning their lessons from "history," the intellectuals—however unintentionally—helped rationalize a status quo largely determined by one man. Dayan's ability to become the sole actor on the scene between 1967 and 1973 can be at least partly attributed to the lack of critical discourse after the victory. Once the intellectuals agreed to derive political lessons from "the situation" (or rather some transcendental version of it), their contribution could not go much beyond a rationalization of that situation. For instance, Dayan's intuition led him to wait for the Arab side, defeated in the war, to come forward and take the peace initiative. This seems inconceivable from the perspective of world history, but very few intellectuals were applying any such perspective to the situation.

The role played by the intellectuals carried certain rewards. Above all, it implied an end to the isolation suffered by those who used independent and deliberate words. It meant a reassertion of the intellectuals' commitment to the community. The following words of one teacher demonstrate how strong the urge to belong had been and how much the Six Day War fulfilled that urge: "A marvellous feeling swept over us all during the Six Day War and throughout those tense days preceding it," he wrote in a teachers' publication. "The threatened danger to our existence roused within us a sense of belonging to one single family, each dependent upon the other, each sensing the other's suffering and participating in each other's joys and anxieties."

Describing the war solidarity as "heartwarming" and hinting that it brought a fresh spirit into a country suffering from many undesirable features, that teacher provided an interesting analogy: "Just as it is during the High Holidays, when the earnest desire to absolve oneself before God purifies the accumulated dross of the past year, and clears away those barriers between people, so these days of struggle stirred the very depths of our hearts with the hope for a purer life without any resentment or suspicion." And he added, "strains of music, harmonious and clear, played on high."[65]

*Chapter Five*

# The Critical Balance

## The Public Dialogue After 1967

The long tradition emphasizing the hope of peace over the glory of war has never changed in Israel. Even the great victory in the Six Day War did not make Israel's poets into warmongers. To the contrary, the books and picture albums flourishing after the war all share a common motive—pride in the victory reached by an army composed mainly of reserves who were forced to abandon their civilian tasks in order to defend the country. To such an army, the joy of triumph is always accompanied by sorrow over the price of victory. Indeed, the most spoken-about publication after the war was a collection of interviews with young soldiers who expressed compassion for the victims of war on the other side of the border. As Chief of Staff Yitzhak Rabin expressed it at the time, "It may be that the Jewish people has never learned and never accustomed itself to feel the triumph of conquest and victory, with the result that these are accepted with mixed feelings."[1]

Israel's intellectuals generally have not shared certain features (such as chauvinism, militarism, and disregard for the enemy) found in other cultures under similar conditions. Nor had the Six Day War brought about an extraordinary amount of hero worship. There were writings that showed admiration for selected generals, but the heroes were portrayed more as reluctant soldiers than as eager officers. They were never described as "greater than life," as were some victorious generals in World War II.[2] So apparent was the lack of hero worship in Israeli literature that in 1975 one scholar complained about the "phony existentialism"[3] of Israel's writers. Israelis, he wrote with a measure of regret, must derive their models of heroism from the literature of other societies.

It would thus be wrong to accuse Israel's intellectuals of betrayal; they betrayed neither the cause of peace nor the cause of critical humanism. They never became conscious ideologues who rationalize—uncritically—existing political positions. However, I would like to argue that the messianic response to the war, described in the previous chapter, had a stagnating effect on the nature of intellectual dialogue in the country. That dialogue had not ceased. Shortly after the war, intellectuals began to express themselves about the desired political settlement and especially about the fate of the occupied territories. The year following the war was labeled the "year of the writers" because of the many political debates in which they participated. But the dialogue took place within defined boundaries set in June 1967 and never truly exceeded them.

By "dialogue" I refer to the Socratic exchange of ideas in society in which common assumptions are treated with skepticism and are critically examined. The dialogical principle, made a cornerstone in the thinking of philosopher Martin Buber,[4] assumes that a continuous critical examination of political issues is a precondition of democracy as well as of political effectiveness and innovativeness.[5] Israel's intellectuals always remained committed to the continuance of dialogue, and they expressed their fear that the failure to examine critically political options may result in disaster. From the perspective of twenty years, however, it can be shown that what at the time seemed an open dialogue was often confined to modes of thought determined by the Six Day War or, rather, by the way it was perceived by the intellectuals.

In October 1973, Israel was caught unprepared when a surprise attack was launched by Egypt and Syria. Much has been written about the preconceptions that prevented Israeli policymakers from suspecting the coming attack.[6] Scholars made insightful comments about the "strategic surprise" and its relationship to similar incidents, such as Pearl Harbor and Operation Barbarossa. They neglected, however, to consider their own role in the development of misleading conceptions.[7] This was the result of a certain intellectual stagnation after the glorious events of 1967. Like generals thinking about the next war in terms of the former, intellectuals failed to apply critical notions to the political scene, even when they thought they did. Such behavior is a recipe for being surprised.[8]

Before I set out to describe the role of intellectuals after the Six Day War, I would like to make the following point. In the soul searching after the 1973 surprise attack, there was a tendency to make distinctions between saints and sinners among the intellectuals. Here I am concerned with the nature of intellectual dialogue in the country, which allows no such distinction. Recently, literary critic Dan Miron published an analysis of a public statement of September 22, 1967, which became the founding document of the Movement for a Greater Israel. The document demanded adherence to the concept of a Greater Israel, which, the statement contended, no government is entitled to give up.

Miron noted the large number of writers, especially older ones, who had signed a document subordinating the sovereign state of Israel and its democratic institutions to an abstract ideal. He explained it by the underlying struggle between two cultures—the "prestate culture" and the "state culture."[9]

According to Miron, the writers who signed the public statement represented the spiritual world of the prestate years, whereas no writer who matured in the state could have supported it. The support given to the statement by War of Independence writers, such as Moshe Shamir and Haim Gouri, Miron explained by arguing that the latter spoke a language that was not in tune with the generation growing up in the sovereign state. Not only is this argument untrue—Shamir and Gouri are read and cherished in modern Israel no less than S. Yizhar and Avraham Shlonsky, who did not sign the statement—but the struggle between two cultures that was envisioned by Miron never took place. Israel's intellectuals had difficulty in coping with the phenomenon of statehood, and the younger generation was no exception; it shared in the messianic response to the Six Day War and in the transcendental public dialogue that followed.

Moreover, though it is correct to stress the role of writers in subordinating the sovereign state of Israel to abstract concepts such as "the Greater Israel," theirs was only a partial role. Writers are known for their messianic tendencies; it was far more significant when scholars— supposedly engaged in cool analysis of options for the Middle East— were entangled in notions whose relevance to reality was no greater than that of the Messiah. Whether conducted by writers, scholars, or teachers, the public dialogue that took place after the war of 1967 had three characteristics: (1) it lacked an element of skepticism, (2) it had  confused strategic and political considerations, and (3) it was very self-centered.

## The Role of Skepticism

The line between self-confidence and overconfidence is thin, but intellectual dialogue can prevent a society from becoming overconfident. After great victories, it is natural for the victor to view the world from the position of strength. The intellectual who applies skepticism under any conditions may thus assist strategic planners by reminding them that conditions are changing and that one's fortunes do not last forever. In moments of national euphoria, the skeptic who casts doubt on truisms and applies the universal lessons of history to a situation considered unique by everybody else plays a thankless but functional role. Skeptics are needed in order to remind a society of the constraints it must consider, especially at a time in which all constraints seem to have been overcome. The skeptic's capacity to cast doubt allows us to endow the intellectual with "foresight," as C. P. Snow said.[10] Intellectuals have no better strategic insights than military experts or politicians have; their foresight comes from the special perspective of the skeptical mind that examines notions about reality even when such examination seems out of tune with the national mood or interest. After the 1967 victory, however, intellectuals were not eager to resume their role as skeptics. To the contrary, the war was seen as having proved old national truisms that could now be pursued in greater confidence.

This was particularly apparent in symposia held by teachers after the war in which its "lessons" were debated. They held many symposia because no other group was as perplexed by the results of the Six Day War as the teachers were. They needed an explanation of the young people's willingness to sacrifice their lives in the name of national values they allegedly lacked. For instance, just a few months before the war, the whole educational system was outraged over a politician's finding that students she interviewed considered "homeland" a rhetorical term, refrained from hero worship, and could not write the first stanza of the national anthem.[11] But then came the war, and the youth proved everybody wrong—eighteen-year-old soldiers who did so poorly in the surveys saved the Jewish people from annihilation, and—most important—did so consciously. They shared in the anxieties and fears that the nation was experiencing and they shared in the sense of fraternity generated by the war.

The teachers had no doubt that the extraordinary performance of the youth in the war must be attributed to the educational system. In their rhetoric, Israel won the war not because it was better equipped and trained but because its youth were endowed with the right values. How could this be reconciled with former complaints over the youth's normlessness? The explanation was simple. The image of the youth as lacking values was a false image disseminated by academia: "Researchers in universities and outside them will perhaps be more careful in the future with rash conclusions about the character of the youth and its teachers' failure," one teacher wrote.[12]

Whoever was responsible for the false image of the youth, one thing was clear to every teacher: The educational system must disseminate national values (as teachers always demanded), but with greater confidence and assertiveness and without letting cloistered academics stand in the way. This point came up again and again. Teachers, who were treated as anachronisms for several years, whose enthusiasm was met with cynicism, whose concern for values was met with laughter, whose grandiloquent language was taken for empty rhetoric, now knew the nightmare was over. It was time ("tomorrow morning" they would say in their meetings) to equip the pupils with Jewish consciousness and with such notions as "the sense of eternity" without shame or guilt. There was no longer any place for doubt and hesitation.

In one symposium, a teacher named Zvi Galon claimed he was possessed with mystical feelings that freed him from any inner conflicts. These conflicts had characterized the era before the war, when teachers knew they were "the last generation of slavery and the first of redemption" but did not admit it wholeheartedly because they were still imprisoned in a mentality of slaves. We were looking for all kinds of justifications for our existence in the country, said Galon, but the Six Day War set the background for a new approach—one of freeing the youth from any guilt over their existence here.

Galon gave several examples of the way he intended to teach literature in the future:

> When I teach Bialik's "On the Slaughter" I shall not limit myself to a presentation of that sense of loss and tragic despair which enveloped the poet when he wrote: "Yours is the powerful arm and ax/Mine the earth entire as execution block" but I shall lead them to the resolution given in Tchernichovsky's "Mine Is the Melody": "And you shall raise a building/for the generation that raises after you, the forthcoming one!"

Galon promised he would stress the message of Nathan Alterman in his collection *City of Doves*: "Then spake she to the lad: The blood/ About the feet of mothers will flood/Yet sevenfold shall the people stand/if defeated upon its very own land." And he added that the following lines of Uri Zvi Greenberg in his book *The Streets of the River,* which he once thought should not be taught, he now grasps in a totally new light: "Tears and torment are in vain/If this wailing does not turn/Into iron ram and horns." "The iron ram is our tank force," said Galon, "and the horns extending forward are our air force."[13]

The new situation in the Middle East, brought about by the military victory, had not been perceived as requiring reassessment and reevaluation. To the contrary, the victory reinforced old notions and ended all hesitations and inner conflicts. To Galon and many others, Israel's right to exist in a land claimed by two peoples would no longer be an issue to be debated in the classroom but a truism proved by the victory. Heated debates took place in the country at times, but they lacked a true element of doubt. For instance, when the controversy began over the exact location of Israel's "secure boundaries," intellectuals took part in it without questioning whether this concept, part of the diplomatic jargon, had any meaning at all. After all, the degree of security a boundary provides depends only partly on its location; it depends above all on the demographic, economic, and military setup in its environment.[14]

Most significantly, very few intellectuals doubted the assumption of Israel's strength. Behind all the options raised after the war lay the assumption that Israel's power was assured for years. Reluctant to reexamine this assumption with time, the intellectuals failed to read the handwriting on the wall. The Six Day War did not end in six days but continued, in the form of a hard and deadly war of attrition, for almost three years. The war of attrition indicated that the Arabs did not consider the defeat as final and were willing to sacrifice their people's lives and welfare for the sake of revenging it. Moreover, the war of attrition indicated that Egypt's great advantage in heavy artillery could, under certain conditions, match Israel's advantages in the battlefield and that it had a great capacity to recover—militarily and politically—from defeat.

This situation did not change the intellectuals' overconfidence. They paid tribute to all the right statements—that reality must be observed in new light, that one should not fight the former war, and so on, but they also resorted to a limited number of truisms: that the Egyptian soldier is unmotivated,[15] that the cease-fire lines of June 1967 "assure us from a surprise attack by our enemies,"[16] that the Arabs would not be willing to negotiate peace in the foreseeable future (hence the territorial and political status quo ought to be maintained),[17] that there is no chance of peace between Israel and Egypt,[18] and that the Palestinian Arabs will somehow adjust to the occupation.[19] One reads the lists of truisms proven wrong and wonders how many mistakes could have been prevented had the intellectuals applied a bit more skepticism in their learned analyses and stated with a little less confidence such conclusions as the following: "It became clear that the control of the Arab states over Europe's sources of oil is none but a political scarecrow, that the Suez Canal is no longer crucial to the world economy, that the Amman government is incapable of conducting an independent policy . . . etc."[20]

### Strategic Thinking

One of the reasons that the intellectuals erred so embarrassingly in their assessments was their tendency to play a role for which they were not equipped—the role of strategic thinkers. After the Six Day War, many intellectuals went from being political critics to being strategic experts, who divided territories, drew borders, and moved armies on paper. The political critic plays a useful role by nature of the questions he raises, but the intellectual who constructs strategic solutions without experience or expertise ends up as a subject of ridicule. Some of Israel's best scholars fell into this trap in the year following the war. There was a long tradition of scholars expressing themselves on national issues in newspapers, but no one ever expected scholars to prove themselves as experts on the specific issues they dealt with. Scholars, like other intellectuals, are invited to express their views because of their capacity to throw light on current issues, ask critical questions about them, and put them in perspective. However, once they cease asking political questions and begin to propose strategic solutions, the question of expertise becomes relevant. Why should the historian, jurist, or political scientist be heard more than any corporal on matters of military strategy? Of what use is their scholarship if they operate within the perspective set by the generals, anyway?

The line between strategic and political thinking is not always clear. Here I refer to the tendency to approach the matter of coexistence between Jews and Arabs in the Middle East by almost exclusive reference to the sphere of military security. One raises questions about "the future," but the future is stripped of its political variables and is treated in terms of the desired location of the Israeli Defense Forces (IDF). Solutions are proposed for the Middle East, but these consider the division of territories between rival armies rather than the desires of people living in those territories. Above all, strategic assumptions are taken as givens that deserve no scrutiny. One such assumption was that time was on Israel's side. This assumption stems from the military mind, which considers time an advantage to any conquering party because it allows it to deepen fortifications, set up military rule, and take care of pockets of resistance. To military planners, it makes sense to ask whether time is on their side, as long as they keep in mind, of course, that the answer depends on what people do with their time. For example, time may be an advantage if one side utilizes it for technological improvement more than the other side.

But the concept makes no sense when applied to international relations. First, the amount and complexity of changes that time might carry is unmanageable. The international scene may change so drastically over time that it is impossible to tell whether these changes will be advantageous. Second, the relative advantage of time cannot be assessed by extrapolation from the military sphere. Although a conquering party may strengthen its control over an occupied population over time, the international situation may change; nationalist feelings may develop, the occupation may cause increasing resistance, the conqueror may lose in international legitimacy, and so on. Israel's scholars, however, often tended to transfer the military clichés to the international scene.

"Time is on our side," wrote Amnon Rubinstein of Tel-Aviv University's law school,[21] "it works for us because we are in charge." Rubinstein, a well-known commentator on current affairs, claimed in an article in the liberal newspaper *Haaretz* that with the passage of time, the new reality created by the IDF turns into a status quo and the status quo is "the holy cow of international relations in our age." In other words, the ability of the military to establish facts in a given territory is the one rule by which the international system operates. "Facts have normative power," he claimed.

Rubinstein put his faith in the factor of time. With time, the Arabs will understand the magnitude of their defeat, their economic difficulties will increase, and the world will "get used" to the new map in the Middle East. The jurist-turned-strategist had no doubt that the new (military) situation in which the Jordan River became Israel's boundary "provides us with a degree of security we have not known before." As if forgetting he was an intellectual, not a general appointed to make statements in the press, Rubinstein wrote that "if officers are now sitting in Cairo, planning the next move against Israel, they should not be envied." As we now know, officers in Cairo were planning the next move, but the dangers involved were ignored by a mode of thinking in Israel that failed to analyze Egyptian political drives and relied instead on what turned out to be a false sense of military security.

The sense of security provided by the new borders led to paralysis of political creativity. Rubinstein was a sober, intelligent thinker, but his conception of peace was limited by what amounted to amateurish military thinking. He suggested that the new situation in the Middle East called for "new thinking," but one can hardly imagine any new idea that, at that time, had a chance to be accepted by him. Any peace treaty reached as a result of Israeli withdrawal to its old boundaries was unacceptable to Rubinstein. The boundaries were so important to him that he ruled out even an almost utopian vision of peace that might bring about commercial relations, tourism, and so on between the countries. "Who could assure us that such a treaty not be violated as the cease fire agreements were violated?" he asked.

This is not to say that Israel's intellectuals ever gave up the search for peace. Once the slightest chance for peace opened up, as during the Sadat initiative of 1977, they called for far-reaching concessions to be made by Israel. But their thinking about peace was not particularly creative, as became clear during the negotiations with Sadat when Israel demanded "normalization" (seen as a strategic asset) but had no plans on how to put the term into operation. The universities could provide little expertise on the subject; their students were much more exposed to "strategic studies" than to peace research. Strategy was something to plan; peace was something to wait for.

## Observing the Environment

In Jewish folklore, there are many stories about a community in which irrelevant debates take place while the world outside is burning. Such folklore developed among people who were aware that they had no real control over their destiny. In a sovereign state, such behavior is disastrous. The state, whose citizens' fate depends on its own decisions rather than on those of others, must constantly observe its environment (defined in real, spatial, and temporal terms rather than messianic ones) and consider its position vis-à-vis that environment. One of the characteristics of the public dialogue held in Israel between the wars of 1967 and 1973 was its lack of such consideration. The victory in the Six Day War resulted in an extraordinary insensitivity to the environment, which subsequently led to all sides in the debate—Left and Right—barricading themselves in grand visions for the Middle East, visions whose applicability was quite small.

At that time, insensitivity to the environment could be found among people who were otherwise very sensitive. For example, the young author Yael Dayan, stationed as military correspondent in the Sinai Desert, noted the corpses rotting along the road, as frequent as telephone poles. But at the same time she welcomed "the space, the absence of people, the heat, the desert wind." The observation of the occupied territories in a romantic mood—ignoring their real sights—was apparent when the sights consisted not only of dead corpses but of living people as well: "We drove to Jericho, the Dead Sea, Kalia. Childhood memories. Refugees crossing the bridge to return to Jordan, Jericho grapes and red flame trees, the main square, the shut doors, soldiers resting."[22] Yael Dayan must have known that the refugees had not "returned" to Jordan but had left their homes on the West Bank, that the sealed doors of Arab shops in the central square of Jericho signified the beginning of an occupation promising as much trouble to the occupier as to the occupied, and that the soldiers would not rest for long. However, the tendency to ignore reality prevailed.

Intellectuals debated options for Israel that were out of touch with facts and processes taking place in the environment. Consider the "Canaanite" option. The Canaanites, as a small group of intellectuals active in prestate Israel was called, revived in 1967 their idea of establishing in the territories under Israeli control a secular Hebrew-speaking entity that would provide equal rights to all its citizens and would align with all other minorities in the Middle East.[23] They failed to explain why the two nations in the area—Jews and Palestinian Arabs—would be willing to give up their nationalities for the sake of the new entity. Visions of the future that were expressed by opponents of the Canaanites were, however, no less remote from reality. Author Haim Be'er, for instance, provided a learned analysis of whether it was in Israel's interest to live in peace and face the risk of cultural assimilation in its environment, or whether it was better to keep living in tension with the environment, which might strengthen processes of national integration.[24] One commentator, trying to answer this question, emphasized the concern throughout the world (including the Arab world) with social and technological progress. He claimed that the state of Israel is the only entity in the Middle East that comes close to the model of a modern welfare state, and therefore Israel might enjoy great prestige among the Arabs and have an enormous influence in the Middle East.[25]

A person in favor of peaceful coexistence in the Middle East might go along with this argument. However, it is based on wrong assumptions. The writer characterized the Palestinian Arab culture as a rural one undergoing a process of urbanization, and he assumed that the Palestinian Arabs' vision of the modern, technological, welfare state might overpower their nationalist drives. However, the Palestinian culture could hardly be characterized as rural and Palestinian nationalism, like every nationalism, grew in an urban environment. The Arabs' main encounter with Israeli technology was on the battlefield, and they did not indicate that they were fascinated with Israeli technology or with the achievements of Israel's welfare state. The assumption that the Arab world might strive for coexistence with Israel as a result of its fascination with Israeli technology, entirely based on wishful thinking, indicates how little has changed in the minds of intellectuals in a hundred years as far as observing reality in Palestine. Some Zionist thinkers lived under the illusion that the Arabs might welcome Jewish immigration because it promised progress and prosperity to the region.[26] That illusion was hidden behind newspaper items such as the one that described Arabs who, after the unification of Jerusalem in 1967, applauded when they first saw modern street lights.[27] Notwithstanding the elitist tone attached to such a story, it reflects disregard for and misunderstanding of the Palestinian national feelings.

Shortly after the 1967 war, some intellectuals began to warn that the Palestinians could not be ignored in any Middle East settlement. In September, Yehoshua Palmon, an expert on the region, doubted the wisdom of Moshe Dayan's passive policy of "waiting for a telephone call" from Arab leaders who might want to negotiate peace with Israel. Palmon noted that the Palestinians in the areas under Israeli occupation had actually called and were sending signals.[28] In October, Nathan Yellin Mor, a commentator from the Israeli Left, reminded everyone that the Arabs of the West Bank and Gaza Strip have a will of their own.[29] And in March 1968, Shlomo Avinery wrote that the establishment of a Palestinian state would be an "almost ideal" combination of the legitimate interests of Israel and the national feelings of the Palestinian population. He expected that the proposal to establish such a state would raise lively and useful public debate.[30] The debate, though lively, turned out to be fruitless. Intellectuals brought the issue of a Palestinian state to the public agenda but never pursued it seriously. This option was debated within parameters, which made it a nonoption. Avinery wrote that "in realistic terms, the present Palestinian leadership—to the extent one can read its intentions—is not inclined towards such a solution."[31] He did not propose trying to learn more thoroughly what that leadership's intentions really were.

Scholars familiar with survey research and other methods of learning forgot all about them when it came to observing the Palestinians living just a few miles away from their universities and research institutes. "The interests of whole strata in the Judean and Samarian population are connected with the continued existence of the [Jordanian] kingdom," Avinery concluded without hesitation.[32] And because he took for granted that there was no chance for a political settlement with the Jordanian kingdom, the Palestinian state, that "almost ideal" solution became dependent on imaginary scenarios leading to Jordan's disintegration. If Jordan were to disintegrate, Avinery believed, and were to be divided between Saudi Arabia, Iraq, and perhaps Syria, then a solution could be worked out. In other words, the only solution depended on processes that existed solely in the visions of a handful of intellectuals who divided the Jordanian kingdom in their imaginations. "The disintegration of Jordan, the fall of Hussein and the division of Trans-Jordan between other Arab countries is the only way which might lead the Palestinians to direct confrontation with their destiny—and with Israel."[33]

## The Reassertion of Critical Humanism

The tendency to entertain illusions became a cultural trait after the Six Day War. Visions of peace raised by the political left were just as illusionary as visions of the Greater Israel perpetuated by the political Right. Consider the "Ode to Peace," written by Yaacov Rothblitt. The "Ode," performed by a military singing group, involved loud, rhythmic, and rousing music in the best tradition of the musical *Hair.* In late 1969 it raised great debate; the poet Nathan Alterman asked whether anybody would have addressed Dwight D. Eisenhower's or Bernard

Law Montgomery's troups in El Alemein with a similar message. Others praised the "Ode" as a legitimate response to the "orgy of albums" published after the Six Day War. And teachers were advised to raise questions about its message in class.[34] Only one journalist, Avraham Schweizer, admitted, after seeing the performance, that no one in the audience could have heard the words anyway because the singing group's barking and yelling as well as its use of loud musical instruments created the effect of a South American or African jungle. The performance could perhaps remind one of a madhouse, he wrote, but could hardly represent the longings for peace of people in their right minds.

This argument makes sense even after the words of the "Ode" are considered. "Let the sun rise up now," sang the group, "let the morning shine. Though we shall never more revive, for all your prayers fine. . . . So therefore sing a song to peace, no whispered prayer about it. But better sing that song to peace, in full voice must we shout it." This was one of dozens of similar songs referring to "peace" in the vaguest form. Israeli pop culture joined forces with other artistic fields in which peace was treated without any consideration for the operational meaning of the term, the ways to achieve it, or the costs and obligations it imposes. Although this stipulation may be too much to ask of the artist, it is not too much to ask of those intellectuals who engaged in ostensibly serious debate over the legitimacy of the song's message. Schweizer had perhaps exaggerated when he claimed that the "Ode to Peace" indicated a transformation of Israeli society into insanity, but intellectual dialogue after the Six Day War was indeed often vague, emotional, and dependent more on one's inner drives than on an examination of environmental conditions.

The failure to conduct a critical, political, and open-minded dialogue after the Six Day War facilitated certain developments that soon came to frighten many intellectuals. These developments were discussed by Ofira Seliktar under the label of "new Zionism."[35] Most important was the gradual spread of the normative view that emphasized the moral and religious significance of the West Bank. Some time in the 1970s, the vision of restoring the state of Israel to the biblical boundaries of the Land of Israel apparently superseded instrumental considerations regarding the West Bank. Seliktar rightly considered this transference as part of a broader public shift toward religious values as well as of a transformation toward a less tolerant political culture.

After the Six Day War, and particularly after the Yom Kippur War of 1973, religious movements stepped into the vacuum created by secular intellectuals. National goals were redefined to stress the millenarian claim to the land of Israel, and a new language was designed that consisted of a blend of religious and political elements. Gush

Emunim, a movement committed to Jewish settling of the West Bank, was founded in 1974 and was immediately associated with a new agenda for Zionism, which consisted of a zero-sum view of Israel's relations with the world and heavy reliance on the Almighty. The coming to power in 1977 of the right-wing Likkud block, headed by Menachem Begin, came to symbolize the new agenda. Begin's militant nationalism is well documented and will not be discussed here. What I would like to demonstrate, however, is the awakening of the intelligentsia to the consequences of nationalism as well as to its own role.[36]

It is during this period that the intelligentsia's role becomes so much more complex than critics, such as George Steiner,[37] have been willing to recognize. Israel's intellectuals have become neither nationalists, as suggested by Steiner, nor automatic opponents of Likkud, as often claimed by that party's supporters. On the one hand, the intellectuals' messianism could be seen as an invitation to those who are far more versed in messianic terms to step into Israeli politics. Also, one cannot ignore the role of right-wing ideologues, such as Israel Eldad and Yuval Ne'eman, in helping blur the distinction between religious and strategic or political thinking, especially as regards the occupied territories. On the other hand, Israel's intellectuals had never ceased to ask certain questions that kept the political dialogue— however problematic—alive. One wonders how far Gush Emunim and other right-wing movements could have gone were it not for the continuous need to answer questions derived from intellectual and moral sources different from those guiding them. This is not to say that right-wing movements do not have internal restraints; it would be wrong to attribute to Gush Emunim lower ethical standards than those of their opponents. However, the sheer reliance on internal ethical codes (naturally perceived as "universal"), without facing moral arguments from the outside, carries the danger of having one's ethics bound to political interests. This danger is particularly apparent in messianic movements. Self-proclaimed messengers of the Almighty have  often neglected universal moral imperatives in the past.[38]

The capacity of society to keep alive a dialogue between the adherents to different ethical codes is of utmost importance. The two sides may not convince each other, but their exposure to alternative codes and the need to cope with those codes on intellectual and political levels tame their prophetic rage. Keeping tension between differing ethical positions may thus be more functional to the maintenance of a social structure than the tension between intellectuals and the powers. Even during the months of euphoria following the victory of 1967, some intellectuals began to raise questions that ultimately had to be coped with. For example, the public statement signed by the great figures of

Israeli literature in support of the concept of "a Greater Israel" raised the question of the fate of the inhabitants of the West Bank. "But they are here," S. Yizhar cried out, "about a million Arabs. Inhabitants and refugees. And they have their own ideas about their future and the territories in which they live."[39]

The intellectuals' realization that the situation may have been more complex than the contenders of differing solutions considered gave rise to a set of fundamental questions that could not be ignored for long. Yizhar was entangled in the same half-baked strategic ideas as were his colleagues. But he also asked what rights a victory gives to the victor in the battlefield, what justifications one can have for the settlement of land by force, and whether it is possible to occupy lands inhabited by others and remain morally untouched. These questions concerning the difficult moral dilemmas of Zionism were put on the agenda again, first hesitantly and then confidently.

In 1970 the historian Jacob Talmon completed a treatise called "Israel Among the Nations." In an attempt to put the Six Day War in historical perspective, he analyzed at length the Zionist movement, its origins, ideas, and deeds. The treatise showed that even the foremost historian is not immune to the grand misconceptions of his era. "Should full scale hostilities be resumed," he wrote, "there is little doubt that the Israeli troops would seize Damascus, enter Cairo, and conquer Amman in no time." This pathetic assumption, however, leads to an important set of questions: "But what next? Could they stay there? And even if they could, what would be the point of it? Is there any certainty that a fourth Jewish victory will at last drive home 'the lesson' to the Arabs?"[40] Talmon was probably wrong in believing that "few people in Israel nourish any illusions on this point."[41] Intellectuals often tend to generalize from their encounter with other intellectuals about the view of the "people." By the time this was written in 1970, there were already more people than Talmon realized who, as a result of the war of attrition, had lost belief in a peaceful solution to the conflict in the Middle East.

But even the most faithful believers in military force as the only means of problem solving in the region could not fully ignore Talmon's message: "Israel may be able to win and win, and go on winning till its last breath, thereby demonstrating the truth of Hegel's aphorism about the 'impotence of victory.' After every victory we would face more difficult, more complicated problems. For as Nietzsche has put it, there are victories which are more difficult to bear than defeat."[42] This scenario was often recalled after the Yom Kippur War, when it came true. In 1973 a surprise attack was launched by Egypt and Syria against Israel, which was able to counter it only after great efforts and after paying a very heavy price. Israel's military victory could not be translated into a political victory, and it became clear that this would be the pattern from now on. Many Israelis felt discouraged and began soul searching. The war was likened to an earthquake that had shaken old notions and provided a starting point for new thinking.

Contrary to the common view, however, the Yom Kippur War did not spark public dialogue; the extreme despair that replaced the euphoria of the prewar years did not encourage an exchange of ideas. Much was written about the decline of social responsibility, the overconfidence of leaders, the materialistic values that took over after 1967, and of course, about the decline in the youth's identification with society.[43] But Left and Right were barricaded in old positions. The need to retreat from some territories conquered in 1967 did not alter the idea of religious circles that considered that conquest a beginning of redemption. And the Left, quite radicalized after the war, had not become more explicit about its program for peace.

A fruitful dialogue began once it became clear, with the formation of Gush Emunim, the weakening of the Labor government, and the rise of Likkud to power in 1977, that two cultures were developing in Israel. To the intellectuals, the perception that a transformation was taking place in the 1970s from labor Zionism, which stressed humanistic and social-democratic values, into a "new Zionism," which stressed national-religious ones was alarming. Most intellectuals were not devoted supporters of Labor: They played a role in its 1977 loss when many members of the intelligentsia, though not voting for Likkud, voted for the Democratic Movement for Change, whose program somewhat resembled that of Rafi. But as we have seen before, the Labor movement represented—in principle—the pioneering spark that had now been adopted by alien forces.

Amos Oz, Israel's renowned writer, living in a kibbutz, admitted in a talk with a Gush Emunim audience that this movement's appearance was a blow to the "standard-bearers." The youth in kibbutzim and the Labor movement, he complained, who as the first generation were accustomed to being looked up to by the country, had now been swindled by the West Bank settlers who adopted their mannerisms and slang. "And although they represented a position far removed from our own, they managed to steal away from us the hearts of some of our spiritual mentors, as if here were the heirs of the pioneering spark that had dimmed."[44] The feeling that the heir apparent had been ousted by the pretender to the throne, a feeling shared by many intellectuals and a major motif in their writing,[45] led them to a reassertion of their role as social critics devoted to an evaluation of society from a universal, humanistic point of view.

The popularity of Oz's *In the Land of Israel* may be understood against this background. The book consisted of a series of encounters—probably a mixture of real and fictitious ones—between the author and members of social groups who expressed viewpoints different from his own. The Orthodox shopkeeper, the beer-drinking fellows in the development town, and the right-wing farmer can all be seen as the troops of new Zionism with the West Bank settlers as the sword's edge. It is the latter with whom Oz was mainly concerned and whom he addressed at length. His message is loud and clear: "When we look at you from a distance, maybe a little sketchily, we see in you a dangerous threat to what is dear and sacred to us. Here the dispute reaches higher than the highest of Samaria's mountains and drops much lower than the lowest point in the Jordan Valley rift: you threaten to boot Israel out of the union between Jewish tradition and Western humanism."[46]

This idea became the main message of Israel's intelligentsia. It consisted of negative and positive dimensions. On the negative side, it feared the fundamentalist conception that reduces all of Judaism to the level of religious ritual and concentrates the ritual on the claim to the land. On the positive side, it defined Judaism as a civilization whose development is coupled with the norms of Western humanism and demands that Jewish nationalism, however challenged, should adhere to those norms. Oz defined the rendezvous between the Jew and Western humanism as irrevocable. He recognized in European humanism, particularly in its liberal and socialist forms, astounding similarities to Jewish imperatives such as "do not do unto others what you would not have others do unto you." Here was a clear reassertion of the tie between Jewish nationalism and the European humanistic experience to which it related from its birth. "Nobody will force us to choose—because we will refuse to make such a choice—between our Judaism and humanism," said Oz to the Gush Emunim settlers who considered the tie artificial. "For us they are one and the same."[47]

It is not clear what Oz had in mind when he proposed that the tie between Jewish nationalism and Western humanism had spiritual offspring in the Hebrew arts. After all, Hebrew art has never come to terms with its own identity, let alone its ties with other civilizations. But in response to nationalist trends developing in the 1970s, intellectuals were willing to state an alternative—one they knew would be quite unpopular in Begin's Israel. The Begin era was characterized by defiance of that tie between Jewish nationalism and Western humanism. Israel's relations with the outside world were defined as hopelessly hostile, a direct extension of the Jew's relationship with an antisemitic Europe and of the Holocaust. Ben-Gurion's ideology, which conceived

Jewish sovereignty as an answer to the persecutions of the past (symbolized in his decision to bring Adolf Eichmann to trial in the courts of the sovereign Jewish state in 1961), was replaced by an ideology promoting the tools of statehood, especially military tools, as means of strengthening the state's position in a situation that had not changed, in principle, since the days of the ghetto.

Begin often gave the impression that he was still living in the Jewish ghetto, fighting off pogroms, as when he associated Yasser Arafat encircled in Beirut with Hitler in his Berlin bunker. Begin's constant references to the Holocaust and his emotional speeches against German Chancellor Helmut Schmidt and other world leaders represented a disbelief that Jewish nationalism would have a chance to interact with its environment. Begin's environment always remained hostile, a factor that had great appeal among social strata that viewed the world in that light. It was also a source of strong mutual hostility between Begin and the intelligentsia. Intellectuals who reached adulthood in the state of Israel after independence have never viewed themselves as fighting off historical persecutors. To them, Jewish nationalism was not only an escape from antisemitism but also a political movement developing as part of nineteenth-century European nationalism. They were very conscious of the Holocaust and the need to prevent it from happening again, but they refused to conceive it as the only model of Israel's relations with the world. Although the threats Israel faced in 1967 and 1973 strengthened their identification with the fate of persecuted Jews throughout history, they still believed that life in a sovereign state puts Israelis in a position allowing interaction with the environment and their cultural heritage.

However, the intelligentsia's perception of the nation-state as a source of relative security did not imply its sanctification. To the contrary, it was defined as "a tool, an instrument, that is necessary for a return to Zion."[48] It may not have been the whole truth when Oz said he did not take pride in the tools of statehood but simply considered them a necessary evil. Israeli intellectuals, being part of their society, often expressed pride in the tools and symbols of statehood, such as the army. But their clear message, sharpened during the war in Lebanon, was that these tools and symbols should not be abused. In June 1982, the Begin government initiated an invasion of Lebanon. The motives guiding Begin to launch the war, in which 600 Israeli soldiers were killed, were seen by many members of the intelligentsia as those of a megalomaniac representing a peripheral subculture asserting its new power.[49] Begin's success in mobilizing the masses in support of the war, which culminated in the harassment of antiwar demonstrators (many of whom were intellectuals), indicates that the subculture Begin represented was no longer located in the periphery. For the intellectuals, however, it always remained peripheral. The "new Zionism" was seen as a distortion, an accident in the development of Israeli society, a nightmare one hoped would be over in the morning.

The war in Lebanon thus gave rise to a series of scholarly works on the limits of power. In the early years of statehood, intellectuals were preoccupied with ethical questions. The new experience of statehood called for an attempt to define moral rules and constraints for the state. For instance, philosophers debated at length about the morality of reprisal actions taken by a sovereign state.[50] However, the unethical nature of the Lebanon War was so clear to the intelligentsia that it hardly raised debate along these lines. The most common question from an ethical point of view was not whether Israel had the right, for instance, to launch a massive bombardment of Beirut—there was almost total agreement among intellectuals that this action was outrageous. It concerned the right to object to illegal orders, as some soldiers did; even this debate was mild. The Lebanon War raised questions mainly of a more "practical" nature. Intellectuals began to wonder whether the Jewish nation-state had a chance at all.

It is no coincidence that scholars who commented on the Lebanon War returned to the myths developed in the early years of the Zionist movement; it was in the muddy terrain of Lebanon that Jewish nationalism had to confront its own myths.[51] Do we want to be like Samson, the bully who relied on his physical strength to the bitter end? Should Bar-Kokhba's courage be cherished by the educational system in spite of the senselessness of his rebellion against the Roman Empire? What is the fate of the lion who gave up the adaptive qualities of the fox? With its modern, well-equipped army stuck in a foreign land as a result of political ambition, manipulation, and fraud, Israel faced very timely questions. The intellectuals who discussed them were accused of "myth breaking," but their concern was genuine. As the title of one book suggested, the Zionist dream had been revisited.[52]

The most important book written during the war in Lebanon was probably Yehoshafat Harkabi's *The Bar-Kokhba Syndrome*. Harkabi, a former head of intelligence and professor of international relations, looked into what he considered an unrealistic attitude repeatedly emerging in Jewish history. He concentrated on the Bar-Kokhba rebellion of A.D. 132–135, in which the Jews who remained in the land of Israel after the great rebellion of A.D. 70 rose against the powerful Roman Empire. The rebellion, whose failure had been foreseen by second-century intellectuals, resulted in destruction, exile, and human suffering. Harkabi analyzed it as an illustration of unrealistic thinking.

Harkabi set the tone for a handful of writings that stressed the need to return from messianic fantasies to reality. He tackled the common assumption that attributed great deeds to the willingness to surpass the boundaries of the possible. A common truism in Israel was that the state's very existence could be attributed to the willingness of its founders to operate against all odds and to ignore reality in the name of burning vision. This truism became a major theme in Gush Emunim's propaganda. But Harkabi objected. Ignoring reality is a blueprint for disaster, he felt. The limits to action must be recognized. A nation's success depends on its realism, that is, its capacity to recognize its abilities as well as its limits. This is what the Jewish proverb "Know thyself" really means.

One chapter in *The Bar-Kokhba Syndrome* is particularly interesting. It is concerned with the question of why Jewish sages in ancient times did not deal more extensively with the Bar-Kokhba rebellion. The rebellion was referred to only occasionally in the literature of the period, and no fundamental analysis was made of the disaster, which was the greatest one in Jewish history to that day. Harkabi explained the absence of analysis as an effort by the sages to ignore the rebellion either because they felt uncomfortable about their support of it or because they regretted their failure to prevent it. Is it possible, Harkabi asked, that by their silence, the sages hoped to prevent complaints by the people? Did they perhaps fear that an open debate would raise second thoughts about the nation's sanity and public morale would drop?

The message to the Israeli intelligentsia was clear: Speak out! When the invasion of Lebanon had started on June 6, 1982, there was no immediate response from the intellectuals. For instance, Amos Oz, a major spokesman for those objecting to the war, did not publish his first article referring to it until June 21. For a short while, people followed the dictum that political criticism should be withheld when the nation was at war. That rule was violated once it was realized that the intellectuals' silence might legitimize an operation representing everything the intellectuals objected to, that is, crude power, lack of concern for human lives, and an unrealistic approach. The need to speak out became an important motif in the poems written during the war. Although some intellectuals remained silent, more and more of them joined the call for self-criticism and self-understanding as a means of avoiding national suicide. In Harkabi's words, "This new situation demands not myths, but sobriety, much self-criticism, and severe criticism of the historical circumstances in which we find ourselves."[53]

During the war in Lebanon, the first in Israeli history fought without a national consensus, the intellectuals explicitly defined their role as that of active critics. Silence was no longer considered an option. Even intellectual groups that lacked a tradition of public service or political involvement stepped into the waters. For instance, legal scholars were known for their preference for the ivory tower. Their tradition had not encouraged them to make political statements unrelated to their field of expertise. However, legal scholars became involved in public affairs in the 1980s, raising their voices in constitutional and political matters.

As one legal scholar, Mordechai Kremnizer, put it, the legal system is not an end in itself. It is a means to assure the conditions for a dignified human life and social justice. Thus, the legal scholar has a commitment to those values and to their dissemination. Legal scholarship must examine the country's legal system as well as social reality. When a state law is found to limit freedom of speech, for example, the scholar has the duty to speak up. Kremnizer called for a "fighting legal academia" and claimed that the moral profile of society is determined not only by those who lead it but also by those who support it with their silence. He felt that scholars have a particular responsibility to voice political criticism when necessary because of their independent status vis-à-vis the government.[54]

Shulamith Hareven, whose willingness to "close the book" in 1967 was pointed out above, wrote an article in 1986 titled "The Role of the Intellectual."[55] She expressed her contempt for "court poets" who uncritically support the status quo and for intellectuals who make high normative statements without getting further involved. Both types, she wrote, fit Benjamin Disraeli's uncomplimentary definition of the intellectual as a person who, when faced with a choice between going to paradise or reading a book about paradise, would prefer the book. Hareven called upon intellectuals to get involved. They should provide society with cognitive dissonance about common truisms. They should tell the public that what it believes to be true may be untrue already or will be in a short while. Such concern over the truth is part of their work as intellectuals. Moreover, they should educate themselves and the public to think in terms of alternatives. The war in Lebanon, wrote Hareven, was a typical anti-intellectual operation because no alternatives and costs were considered. The intellectual should bring to the government's attention some options for change as well as information about who would pay the price of the war.

Hareven realized that political involvement did not promise the intellectuals a rose garden, but she still insisted that they not refrain from re-examining national myths. In the Begin era, the perpetuation of myths, such as that of Bar-Kokhba, took on a rather direct and crude form. Teachers had never been too critical about the consequences of the Bar-Kokhba rebellion, and generations of students were exposed exclusively to its heroic dimensions. But even the most devoted teacher could not remain silent when, in May 1982, Begin arranged an official ceremony in which human bones found in the Judean Desert were declared to be those of Bar-Kokhba's lieutenants and were given a state burial.

Myths, wrote Hareven, must be "humanized," that is, put to constant examination from a daily, human perspective. The intellectuals must ask questions about their substance and reveal their misuse. This is where intellectuals would be at their best, she believed, because their occupation consists of examination and interpretation. Hareven did not have in mind myth breaking for its own sake. Like other intellectuals, she called for a resumption of the lost perspective of critical humanism. In taking up this perspective, the intelligentsia demonstrated a high degree of maturity. They were aware that their political criticism should not be detached from reality. Israel's intellectuals took precautions to avoid suffering the fate of the European or U.S. New Left, which, in the 1970s, found itself isolated and without influence. As analyzed by Aharon Megged, the New Left had no roots within any social class and has always remained a cosmopolitan movement, driven by spontaneous, emotional, and intuitive responses to events. Megged attributed the movement's failure to its lack of doubt, the most important tool of the intellectual. The New Left ceased asking questions, he claimed. Did Mao Tse-tung really represent freedom, as the movement's slogans implied? What was really happening in Fidel Castro's Cuba? And did "black is beautiful" really include Idi Amin's political regime in Uganda?[56]

However one feels about these questions, they carry an important lesson. An intelligentsia that finds itself united on one front, with the government on the other, can easily color the world in black and white and automatically join any act of opposition. Intellectuals can demonstrate or sign petitions not as a result of their critical examination of events but because others do. Israel's intellectuals, however, were quite careful to expose such tendencies once they were identified and to develop self-correcting mechanisms.

For example, Miron Benvenisti, a scholar who studied the situation in the West Bank and often came up with counterintuitive findings, announced in 1982 his conclusion that the gradual integration of the West Bank into Israel's economy came close to a point of no return. Benvenisti's study created considerable cognitive dissonance among intellectuals on the left, for whom the solution to the issue of occupation relied on one form or another of separation between the West Bank and Israel. Although Benvenisti did not escape accusations about his betrayal of the cause, his study became a major point of reference in political debates over the territories.[57] Another example concerns the willingness of four major writers—Yizhar, Oz, Yehoshua, and Gouri—to risk the flak they knew they would get from fellow intellectuals and to voice, in 1984, their support for a national unity government (composed of both the Labor and Likkud parties), which seemed to them the best means of ending the war in Lebanon.

In 1983, the literary scholar Gershon Shaked wrote a review of an autobiography by Israeli historian Saul Friedlander, in which he related his moving experiences in the Holocaust.[58] Shaked, who as a child had been through similar experiences, criticized Friedlander for the minimal space given in the autobiography to his experiences after the establishment of the state of Israel. Shaked saw in the work the attitude of an intellectual elite still longing for the cultural milieu of Europe in which it had played an avant-garde role.[59] Shaked complained that this elite identifies with the state only so long as the latter meets its expectations. However, once the state's "stocks" drop, as happened to Israel's international image during the war in Lebanon, the intellectuals become alienated from it. Shaked titled his article "No Other Place." To him, intellectuals could not separate their own fate from that of the community in which they lived. He compared Friedlander to George Steiner, who longed for a form of Judaism that no longer exists—one associated with cosmopolitan Europe before World War II. But the cosmopolitan world had disappeared, wrote Shaked. It was time to face reality in the state of Israel.

In the Introduction, I defined the role of the intellectual, based on Michael Walzer's definition, as one of "being here and drawing the line." We expected the intellectual to be committed, in Socratic fashion, both to the community and to social critique. The behavior of Israel's intelligentsia in the 1980s can be interpreted as an attempt to reassert this role. Intellectuals resumed the critical perspective, admittedly abandoned in the Six Day War, but at the same time they were very careful not to let this perspective turn into dogma. This forbearance could only be assured by the intellectuals' restraining their messianic tendencies and remaining in touch with reality. It remains to be seen whether they will do this in the future, which promises to hold no fewer challenges for the Israeli intellectual than did the past.

# Notes

## Chapter 1

1. George Steiner, "A Kind of Survivor," *Commentary* 39 (February 1965): 32–38.
2. George Steiner, "Our Homeland, the Text," *Salmagundi* 66 (Winter-Spring 1985): 4–25.
3. See Alexander Altmann, *Moses Mendelssohn: A Biographical Essay* (University: University of Alabama Press, 1973).
4. Jacov Katz, *Out of the Ghetto: The Social Background of Jewish Emancipation, 1770–1870* (Cambridge, Mass.: Harvard University Press, 1973).
5. See William D. Rubinstein, "Jewish Intellectuals in Liberal Democracies." In *Intellectuals in Liberal Democracies: Political Influence and Social Involvement,* edited by Alain Gagnon (New York: Praeger, 1987), pp. 179–198.
6. See Walter Laqueur, *A History of Zionism* (Oxford: Clarendon, 1975); David Vital, *The Origins of Zionism* (Oxford: Clarendon, 1975); David Vital, *Zionism: The Formative Years* (Oxford: Clarendon, 1982); Bernard Avishai, *The Tragedy of Zionism: Revolution and Democracy in the Land of Israel* (New York: Farrar, Straus, Giroux, 1985); and Harold Fisch, *The Zionist Revolution: A New Perspective* (London: Weidenfeld & Nicolson, 1978).
7. Theodor Herzl, *The Jewish State: An Attempt at a Modern Solution of the Jewish Question* (London: Forbes, 1972).
8. Ibid., p. 29.
9. Ibid., p. 78.
10. Isaac Deutscher, "The Non-Jewish Jew." In *The Non-Jewish Jew and Other Essays,* edited by Isaac Deutscher (London: Oxford University Press, 1968), p. 35.
11. The most important expression of this point of view can be found in Franz Rosenzweig, *Der Stern der Erlösung* (Frankfurt: Kaufmann, 1921). See also Nahum Glatzer, *Franz Rosenzweig, His Life and Thought* (New York: Schocken, 1953).
12. Julien Benda, *The Betrayal of the Intellectuals* (Boston: Beacon, 1955), p. 47.
13. Ibid., p. 48.
14. See Meir Mindlin, "Israel's Intellectuals: Young Writers and Middle-Aged Critics," *Commentary* 25 (March 1958): 217–225.

15. Eliahu Tscherikower, *Yehudim Be'itot Mahapecha* (Tel Aviv: Am Oved, 1957).

16. See Vladimir Nahirny, *The Russian Intelligentsia: From Torment to Silence* (New Brunswick, N.J.: Transaction, 1983).

17. Arthur Hertzberg, ed., *The Zionist Idea: A Historical Analysis and Reader* (New York: Atheneum, 1973).

18. Frederic V. Grünfeld, *Prophets Without Honour* (London: Hutchinson, 1979).

19. Lewis S. Feuer, *Marx and the Intellectuals: A Set of Post-Ideological Essays* (Garden City, N.Y.: Doubleday, 1969).

20. Robert Brym, *Intellectuals and Politics* (London: Allen & Unwin, 1980).

21. A striking example concerns the role of Polish intellectuals after the insurrection of 1831. See Roman Dyboski, "Literature and National Life in Modern Poland," *Slavonic Review* 3 (June 1924-March 1925): 117–130; and Wiktor Weintraub, "Adam Mickiewicz the Mystic-Politician," *Harvard Slavic Studies* 1 (1953): 137–178.

22. Lewis A. Coser, *Men of Ideas: A Sociologist's View* (New York: Free Press, 1965).

23. Harold Lasswell, "The World Revolution of our Time: A Framework for Basic Policy Research." In *World Revolutionary Elites: Studies in Coercive Ideological Movements,* edited by Harold Lasswell and Daniel Lerner (Cambridge, Mass.: MIT Press, 1965).

24. Edward Shils, "The Intellectuals and the Powers: Some Perspectives for Comparative Analysis." In *On Intellectuals,* edited by Philip Rieff (Garden City, N.Y.: Doubleday, 1970), p. 32.

25. See, for example, James Wilkinson, *The Intellectual Resistance in Europe* (Cambridge, Mass.: Harvard University Press, 1981); Michael Paul Rogin, *The Intellectuals and McCarthy: The Radical Specter* (Cambridge, Mass.: MIT Press, 1967).

26. Ralf Dahrendorf, *Society and Democracy in Germany* (Garden City, N.Y.: Doubleday, 1967), p. 267.

27. On the ideologue, see Karl Mannheim, *Ideology and Utopia* (New York: Harcourt, 1936); Lewis S. Feuer, *Ideology and the Ideologists* (Oxford: Blackwell, 1975).

28. See, for instance, William Barrett, *The Truants: Adventures Among the Intellectuals* (Garden City, N.Y.: Anchor, 1982); Jane Burbank, *Intelligentsia and Revolution: Russian Views of Bolshevism, 1917–1922* (New York: Oxford University Press, 1986); Merle Goldman, *China's Intellectuals: Advice and Dissent* (Cambridge, Mass.: Harvard University Press, 1981); Paul Hollander, *Political Pilgrims: Travels of Western Intellectuals to the Soviet Union, China, and Cuba 1928–1978* (New York: Oxford University Press, 1981); and Frank Leslie Vatai, *Intellectuals in Politics: The Greek World* (London: Croom Helm, 1984).

29. Talcott Parsons, "'The Intellectual': A Social Role Category." In *On Intellectuals,* edited by Philip Rieff, p. 4.

30. On this point, see Charles Kadushin, *The American Intellectual Elite* (Boston: Little, Brown, 1974).

31. This concept is elaborated in Alvin W. Gouldner, "Prologue to a Theory of Revolutionary Intellectuals," *Telos* 26 (Winter 1975-1976): 3–36.

32. Dahrendorf, pp. 267–268.

33. See, for instance, Régis Debray, *Teachers, Writers, Celebrities* (London: NLB, 1981); Roderic A. Camp, *Intellectuals and the State in Twentieth Century Mexico* (Austin: University of Texas Press, 1985).

34. See Alexander Gella, ed., *The Intelligentsia and the Intellectuals* (Beverly Hills, Calif.: Sage, 1976).

35. Raymond Aron, *The Opium of the Intellectuals* (Garden City, N.Y.: Doubleday, 1957), p. 210.

36. Joseph A. Schumpeter, *Capitalism, Socialism and Democracy* (New York: Harper, 1942), p. 146.

37. J. P. Nettl, "Ideas, Intellectuals, and Structures of Dissent." In *On Intellectuals*, edited by Philip Rieff, p. 60.

38. Dahrendorf. See also Ralf Dahrendorf, "The Intellectual and Society: The Social Function of the 'Fool' in the Twentieth Century." In *On Intellectuals*, edited by Philip Rieff.

39. Dahrendorf, p. 275.

40. Michael Walzer, "The Politics of the Intellectual: Julien Benda's *La Trahison des Clercs* Reconsidered." In *Conflict and Consensus: A Festschrift in Honor of Lewis A. Coser*, edited by Walter Powell and Richard Robbins (New York: Free Press, 1984), pp. 365–377.

41. Ibid., p. 375.

42. Ibid.

43. See Tatsuo Arima, *The Failure of Freedom: A Portrait of Modern Japanese Intellectuals* (Cambridge, Mass.: Harvard University Press, 1969); A. Brand, "Critical Theory in Context: The Political Cabaret of Pre-War German Sociology," *Australian and New Zealand Journal of Sociology* 18 (March 1982): 31–43; Allan J. Matusow, "John F. Kennedy and the Intellectuals," *Wilson Quarterly* 7 (Autumn 1983): 140–153; Paul Clay Sorum, *Intellectuals and Decolonization in France* (Chapel Hill: University of North Carolina Press, 1977).

44. See Noam Chomsky, *Intellectuals and the State* (Baarn, Netherlands: Het Werldvenster Baarn, 1978); Alastair Hamilton, *The Appeal of Fascism* (New York: Avon, 1971); Fritz K. Ringer, *The Decline of the German Mandarins: The German Academic Community, 1890-1933* (Cambridge, Mass.: Harvard University Press, 1969)

45. Leszek Kolakowski, "Intellectuals Against Intellect," *Daedalus* 101 (Summer 1972): 1–15.

46. See Edward Shils, "Intellectuals, Tradition and the Traditions of Intellectuals: Some Preliminary Considerations." In *Intellectuals and Tradition*, edited by S. N. Eisenstadt and S. R. Graubard (New York: Humanities Press, 1973), pp. 27–51.

# Chapter 2

1. See Edward Hallett Carr, *Nationalism and After* (New York: Macmillan, 1945); Hans Kohn, *The Idea of Nationalism: A Study in its Origins and*

*Background* (New York: Macmillan, 1944); Hans Kohn, *Prophets and Peoples: Studies in Nineteenth Century Nationalism* (New York: Macmillan, 1946); and Jacques Barzun, "Cultural Nationalism and the Makings of Fame." In *Nationalism and Internationalism,* edited by Edward Mead Earle (New York: Columbia University Press, 1950), pp. 3–17.

2. William L. Langer, *Political and Social Upheaval, 1832–1852* (New York: Harper & Row, 1969, Chapter 8.

3. Ronald Sussex, "Introduction." In *Culture and Nationalism in Nineteenth-Century Eastern Europe,* edited by Ronald Sussex and J. C. Eade (Columbus, Ohio: Slavica, 1983), p. 3.

4. Ibid., pp. 3–4.

5. See Lilyan Kesteloot, *Intellectual Origins of the African Revolution* (Washington, D.C.: Black Orpheus Press, 1972); Ali A. Mazrui, *Cultural Engineering and Nation-Building in East Africa* (Evanston, Ill.: Northwestern University Press, 1972); Gobinda Prasad Sarma, *Nationalism in Indo-Anglican Fiction* (New Delhi: Sterling, 1978); S. P. Sen, *History in Modern Indian Literature* (Calcutta: Institute of Historical Studies, 1975); Yogendra K. Malik (ed.), *South Asian Intellectuals and Social Change* (New Delhi: Heritage, 1982).

6. Konstantin Symmons-Symonolewicz, *Nationalist Movements: A Comparative View* (Meadville, Pa.: Maplewood, 1970), p. 23.

7. See Ernst Gellner, *Nations and Nationalism* (Ithaca, N.Y.: Cornell University Press, 1983); John Breuilly, *Nationalism and the State* (New York: St. Martin's Press, 1982); and G. L. Mosse, *The Nationalization of the Masses: Political Symbolism and Mass Movements in Germany from the Napoleonic Wars through the Third Reich* (New York: Howard Fertig, 1975).

8. Bernard Lewis, *History—Remembered, Recovered, Invented* (Princeton, N.J.: Princeton University Press, 1975).

9. See Eric Hobsbawn and Terence Ranger, *The Invention of Tradition* (Cambridge: Cambridge University Press, 1983).

10. Hugh Trevor-Roper, "The Invention of Tradition: The Highland Tradition of Scotland." In ibid.

11. Harry Elmer Barnes, *A History of Historical Writing* (New York: Dover, 1962 [1937]), especially Chapter 9.

12. Ibid., pp. 226–228.

13. Shlomo Avinery, *The Making of Modern Zionism: The Intellectual Origins of the Jewish State* (London: Weidenfeld & Nicolson, 1981), Chapter 2.

14. A collection of Dubnow's work appeared in English in Simon Dubnow, *Nationalism and History: Essays on Old and New Judaism* (New York: Atheneum, 1970).

15. See Simon Dubnow, "The Doctrine of Jewish Nationalism." In ibid., pp. 76–99.

16. Simon Dubnow, "The Sociological View of Jewish History" (Introduction to the *Weltgeschichte,* 1925). In ibid., pp. 336–353.

17. Ibid., p. 339.

18. Ibid.

19. Dubnow, "The Doctrine of Jewish Nationalism." In ibid., p. 99.

20. Ahad Ha'am, *Selected Essays,* translated by Leon Simon (Philadelphia, Pa.: Jewish Publication Society, 1912).

21. Ibid., p. 84.

22. Ibid., p. 236.

23. Ibid.

24. Ibid., p. 241.

25. Eliezer Schweid, *The Land of Israel: National Home and Land of Destiny* (London: Associated University Presses, 1985).

26. See Gershom Scholem, *The Messianic Idea in Judaism and Other Essays on Jewish Spirituality* (New York: Schocken, 1971).

27. Avinery, p. 47.

28. Quoted in Schweid, p. 177.

29. See A. D. Gordon, *Selected Essays,* translated by Frances Burnce (New York: League for Labor Palestine, 1938).

30. See, especially, Moses Hess, *Rome and Jerusalem* (New York: Philosophical Library, 1958).

31. Gordon, p. 13.

32. Martin Buber, *On Zion: The History of an Idea* (London: Horovitz, 1973), pp. 147–148.

33. The need to accompany the Zionist effort by works of scholarship had always been part of the Zionist creed. See Theodor Herzl, *Altneuland* (Berlin: Benjamin Harz, 1902).

34. See P. A. Sorokin, *Society, Culture, and Personality* (New York: Harper, 1947); and Elie Kedouri, *Nationalism* (New York: Praeger, 1961).

35. F. M. Barnard, *Herder's Social and Political Thought* (Oxford: Clarendon, 1965), p. 57.

36. Symmons-Symonolewicz, p. 32.

37. Barnard.

38. For a detailed account, see Langer, Chapter 8.

39. Joshua A. Fishman, *Language and Nationalism: Two Integrative Essays* (Rowley, Mass.: Newbury, 1972).

40. Ibid., p. 55.

41. N. H. Tur-Sinai, *The Revival of the Hebrew Language* (Jerusalem: R. H. Hacohen, 1960), p. 8

42. See Scott Saulson, ed., *Institutionalized Language Planning* (The Hague: Mouton, 1979).

43. See Robert St. John, *Tongue of the Prophets: The Life Story of Eliezer Ben Yehuda* (Garden City, N.Y.: Doubleday, 1952).

44. Eliezer Ben-Yehuda, "She'ela Lohata." In *Israel Le'artzo Velilshono,* edited by Ithamar Ben-Avi (Jerusalem: Hassolel, 1929), pp. 3–13.

45. Peretz Smolenskin, "The Haskala of Berlin." In *The Zionist Idea: A Historical Analysis and Reader,* edited by Arthur Hertzberg (New York: Atheneum, 1973), p. 156.

46. "A Letter of Ben Yehuda 1880." In ibid., p. 164.

47. Ibid.

48. Ibid.

49. On the literary renaissance, see Eisig Silberschlag, *From Renaissance to Renaissance: Hebrew Literature from 1492–1970* (New York: Ktav, 1973); and Joseph Klausner, *A History of Modern Hebrew Literature, 1785–1930* (London: M. L. Cailingold, 1932).

50. For excerpts of renaissance writings, see S. Y. Penueli and A. Ukhmani, *Hebrew Short Stories: An Anthology* (Tel-Aviv: Megiddo, 1965).

51. David Patterson, "The Influence of Hebrew Literature on the Growth of Jewish Nationalism in the Nineteenth Century." In *Culture and Nationalism in Nineteenth Century Eastern Europe,* edited by Ronald Sussex and J. C. Eade, pp. 84–95.

52. See especially Abraham Mapu, *The Love of Zion* (Warsaw, 1869).

53. Gershon Shaked, "The Great Transition." In *The Great Transition: The Recovery of the Lost Centers of Modern Hebrew Literature,* edited by Glenda Abramson and Tudor Parfitt (Totowa, N.J.: Rowman & Allanheld, 1985), pp. 117–125.

54. Ibid., p. 122.

55. Gordon, p. 101.

56. Ibid., p. 118.

57. Ibid., pp. 114–115.

58. Ibid., p. 111.

59. Ibid.

60. Ibid., p. 153.

61. Berl Katznelson, "Tarbut Vano'ar Bahistadrut," lecture published by the Federation of Labor, p. 3.

62. See S. N. Eisenstadt, "Intellectuals and Political Elites." In *Intellectuals in Liberal Democracies,* edited by Alain Gagnon (New York: Praeger, 1987), p. 161.

63. See Ruth Miller Elson, *Guardians of Traditional American Schoolbooks of the Nineteenth Century* (Lincoln: University of Nebraska Press, 1964); Frank A. Stone, *The Rub of Cultures in Modern Turkey: Literary Views of Education* (Bloomington: Indiana University Press, 1973).

64. Hans Kohn, *Prelude to Nation-States: The French and German Experiences, 1789–1815* (Princeton, N.J.: Van Nostrand, 1967), p. 77.

65. See L. M. Cullen, "The Cultural Basis of Modern Irish Nationalism." In *The Roots of Nationalism: Studies in Northern Europe,* edited by Rosalind Mitchison (Edinburgh: John Donald, 1980), pp. 101–102.

66. Ahad Ha'am, "The Spiritual Revival." In *Selected Essays,* translated by Leon Simon (Philadelphia, Pa.: Jewish Publication Society, 1912), p. 301.

67. Gordon, p. 95.

68. Ibid.

69. Ibid.

70. See Aharon Kleinberger, *Society, Schools and Progress in Israel* (Oxford: Pergamon, 1969), Chapter 5.

71. See Rachel Dror, *Jewish Education in Israel* (Jerusalem: Yad Ben-Zvi, 1987) (in Hebrew).

72. See Ruth Firer, *The Agents of Zionist Education* (Tel Aviv: Hakibbutz Hameuchad, 1985) (in Hebrew).

73. See also Yonathan Shapiro, *An Elite Without Successors: Generations of Political Leaders in Israel* (Tel Aviv, Sifriyat Hapoalim, 1984) (in Hebrew); and Haim Ormean, ed., *Education in Israel* (Jerusalem: Ministry of Education, 1973) (in Hebrew).

# Chapter 3

1. See A. M. Dharmalingam, *Blasted Hopes or Democracy in India* (Bangalore: The Kural Nilayam, 1951); P. J. Vatikiotis, *Egypt Since the Revolution* (London: Allen & Unwin, 1968); Shatto Arthur Gakwandi, *The Novel and Contemporary Experience in Africa* (London: Heinemann, 1977).

2. On the concept, see Jacob L. Talmon, *Political Messianism: The Romantic Phase* (New York: Praeger, 1960).

3. On disillusionment with messianic schemes, see Tawfiq Al-Hakim, *The Return of Consciousness* (New York: New York University Press, 1985); Cosmo Pieterse and Donald Munro, *Protest and Conflict in African Literature* (London: Heinemann, 1969); Jonathan Peters, *A Dance of Masks: Senghor, Achebe, Soyinka* (Washington, D.C.: Three Continents Press, 1978); and Sylvia Washington Bâ, *The Concept of Negritude in the Poetry of Léopold Sédar Senghor* (Princeton, N.J.: Princeton University Press, 1973).

4. See especially Bruce Robson, *The Drum Beats Nightly* (Tokyo: The Center for East Asian Cultural Studies, 1976); K. R. Srinivasa Iyengar, ed., *Indian Literature Since Independence: A Symposium* (New Delhi: Sahitya Akademi, 1973); and Lewis Nkosi, *Tasks and Masks: Themes and Styles of African Literature* (Essex: Longman, 1981).

5. Alvin W. Gouldner, "Prologue to a Theory of Revolutionary Intellectuals." In *Telos* 26 (Winter 1975-1976): 8.

6. Faiz Ahmed Faiz, "This Harvest of Hopes." In *Poems by Faiz,* translated by V. S. Kiernan (London: Allen & Unwin, 1971), p. 213.

7. See Eldred Durosimi Jones, *The Writing of Wole Soyinka* (London: Heinemann, 1973).

8. Nkosi, p. 68.

9. Quoted in Calude Wauthier, *The Literature and Thought of Modern Africa* (London: Heinemann, 1978), p. 274.

10. See the following speeches: Julius K. Nyerere, "The Intellectual Needs Society." In *Man and Development,* edited by Binadamu Na Maendeleo (London: Oxford University Press, 1974); Tom Mboya, "Kenya Intellectuals and the K.A.N.U. Government." In *The Challenge of Nationhood: A Collection of Speeches and Writings by Tom Mboya* (New York: Praeger, 1970); and Jomo Kenyatta, "University Ceremony—1965." In *Suffering Without Bitterness: The Founding of the Kenya Nation,* speeches by Jomo Kenyatta (Nairobi: East African Publishing House, 1968).

11. An important analysis of this phase can be found in Ali A. Mazrui, *Cultural Engineering and Nation-Building in East Africa* (Evanston, Ill.:

Northwestern University Press, 1972). See also Ali A. Mazrui, *Political Values and the Educated Class in Africa* (London: Heinemann, 1978); and Syed Hussein Alatas, *Intellectuals in Developing Societies* (London: Cass, 1977).

12. For an excellent analysis of this trend, see Chris L. Wanjala, *Standpoints on African Literature: A Critical Anthology* (Nairobi: East African Literature Bureau, 1973).

13. Charles and Barbara Jelavich, *The Establishment of the Balkan National States, 1804–1920* (Seattle: University of Washington Press, 1977).

14. Wanjala, p. 4.

15. Avigdor Hameiri in *Divrey Sofrim,* protocol of a meeting between Ben-Gurion and writers, March 27, 1949, p. 21. Ben-Gurion Archives.

16. See Michael Keren, *Ben-Gurion and the Intellectuals: Power, Knowledge and Charisma* (DeKalb: Northern Illinois University Press, 1983); and Mitchell Cohen, *Zion and State: Nation, Class and the Shaping of Modern Israel* (Oxford: Basil & Blackwell, 1987).

17. See David Ben-Gurion, *Ben-Gurion Looks at the Bible,* translated by Jonathan Kolatch (London: W. H. Allen, 1972).

18. See, for instance, Eliahu Hassin and Dan Horowitz, *Haparashah* (Tel Aviv: Am Hassefer, 1961); and Nathan Yanai, *Qera Batzameret* (Tel Aviv: Levin-Epstein, 1969).

19. See David Ben-Gurion and Nathan Rotenstreich, "Israel and Zionism: A Discussion." *Jewish Frontier* 24 (December 1957); and Shlomo Avinery, "Israel in the Post Ben-Gurion Era: The Nemesis of Messianism," *Midstream* 11 (September 1965): 16–32.

20. For overviews of Israel in the 1960s, see Amos Elon, *The Israelis: Founders and Sons* (London: Penguin, 1983); Charles Liebman and Eliezer Don Yehiya, *The Civil Religion of Israel* (Berkeley: University of California Press, 1984); and Michael Keren, "Intellectuals and the Open Society in Israel." In *Intellectuals in Liberal Democracies: Political Influence and Social Involvement,* edited by Alain G. Gagnon (New York: Praeger, 1987).

21. Nurith Gerth, *Amos Oz* (Tel Aviv: Sifriyat Hapoalim, 1980), p. 9 (in Hebrew).

22. See, for example, Jerome S. Bruner, *The Process of Education* (Cambridge, Mass.: Harvard University Press, 1960).

23. On the Jewish intellectual and commitment, see Simon Halkin, *Modern Hebrew Literature: Trends and Values* (New York: Schocken, 1950).

24. "Ma Mekomo Shel Sofer?" *Moznayim* 18 (March 1964): 231.

25. On generations in Israel's intelligentsia, see Meir Mindlin, "Israel's Intellectuals: Young Writers and Middle-Aged Critics," *Commentary* 25 (March 1958): 217–225.

26. See Gershom Scholem, *Explications and Implications: Writings on Jewish Heritage and Renaissance* (Tel Aviv: Am Oved, 1975) (in Hebrew).

27. Hayim Nahman Bialik, "Revealment and Concealment in Language: Reflections on the Nature of Literature," *Commentary* 9 (February 1950): 171–175.

28. Ibid., p. 172.

29. Ibid., p. 174.

30. Ibid., p. 172.

31. Ibid.

32. The articles were published in the newspaper *Davar* on November 5, 1965; November 12, 1965; November 26, 1965; and December 3, 1965.

33. Ha'academia Lalashon Ha'ivrit, *Zichronot* (Jerusalem: Tel Aviv University Library, 1966).

34. See Dan Miron, *When Corners Come Together* (Tel Aviv: Am Oved, 1987) (in Hebrew).

35. On the War of Independence generation, see Gershon Shaked, *Gal Hadash Bassiporet Ha'ivrit* (Tel Aviv: Sifriyat Hapoalim, 1971).

36. On literary developments in the 1960s, see Leon I. Yudkin, *Escape into Siege: A Survey of Israeli Literature Today* (London: Routledge and Kegan Paul, 1974).

37. Gideon Merav, "Sifrut Uzeramin Ra'ayoniyim," *Achshav* 5-6 (Spring 1959): 253–254.

38. Gavriel Moked, "He'arot Beviku'ah Efshari," *Achshav* 3-4, p. 27.

39. Ibid., p. 30.

40. Ibid., p. 33.

41. Nathan Zach, "Hirhurim Al Shirat Alterman," *Achshav* 3-4, pp. 109–122.

42. Baruch Kurzweil, "Be'ayot Hayetzira Hassifrutit Be'israel," *Moznayim* 23 (July 1966): 126–129.

43. James Diamond, "The Literary Criticism of Baruch Kurzweil," Dissertation, University of Michigan, Ann Arbor, 1984.

44. A. B. Yehoshua, *Three Days and a Child,* translated by M. Arad (New York: Doubleday, 1970).

45. Baruch Kurzweil, "He'arot Lematzav Sifrutenu Besha'a zo," *Haaretz,* September 6, 1964.

46. Amos Oz, "Messarev Ani La'amod Amida Shel Hitbatlut Ekronit," *Moznayim* 23 (July 1966): 133–134.

47. Moshe Dor, "Ani Le'atzmi," *Maariv,* March 27, 1959.

48. Aharon Megged, *The Living on the Dead* (London: Cape, 1970).

49. Oded Be'eri, "Me'aharim Baneshef," *Haaretz,* March 29, 1963.

50. See Ronald Berman, *America in the Sixties: An Intellectual History* (New York: Free Press, 1968).

51. Gideon Katznelson, "Le'an Hem Holchim?" *Moznayim* 12 (April-May 1961): 419–426.

52. Gideon Katznelson, "Kirkassut Bimkom Shira," *Moznayim* 13 (July 1961): 127–129.

53. Moshe Dor, "Nessi'a Lelit," quoted in Gideon Katznelson, "Le'an Hem Holchim?" *Moznayim* 14 (April-May 1962): 404–413.

54. Tuvia Ruebner, "Te'uda," quoted in "Le'an Hem Holchim?"

55. Yitzhak Akaviahu, "Yaacov Avinu Veta'harut Kaduregel," *Moznayim* 19 (November 1964): 523–524.

56. Yehuda Amichai, "Yaacov Vehamalach." In *Shirim* (Tel Aviv: Schocken, 1977).

57. Amir Gilboa, *Kehulim Va'adumim* (Tel Aviv: Am Oved, 1963), p. 346 (in Hebrew).

58. Gideon Katznelson, "Le'an Hem Holchim?" *Moznayim* 19 (August-September 1964), p. 263.

59. Labor party's Central Committee meeting, protocol, June 30, 1960, Ben-Gurion Archives.

60. Ibid. p. 7.

61. Aharon Megged, "Hassifrut Ben Hazemanim," *Daf* 24 (May 1964): 9–12.

62. Ibid., p. 12.

63. Y. Saharoni, "Bigdey Hamelech Be'habima," *Moznayim* 14 (January 1962): 240–241.

64. Joachim Stuschewsky, "Musica Bat Zemanenu Al Parashat Derachim," *Moznayim* 16 (April-May 1963): 436–439.

65. On this pattern, see Harold Lasswell and Daniel Lerner, eds., *World Revolutionary Elites: Studies in Coercive Ideological Movements* (Cambridge, Mass.: MIT Press, 1965).

66. Shalom Levin in Hakeness Hapedagogi (pedagogical conference of the Teachers' Federation), 1960, protocol, AJE 10. 25/738, p. 1.

67. For similar approaches in the world at the time, see Jacques Ellul, *The Technological Society* (New York: Vintage, 1964); and Ralph Lapp, *The New Priesthood: The Scientific Elite and the Uses of Power* (New York: Harper & Row, 1965).

68. Norbert Wiener, *Cybernetics: Or Control and Communication in the Animal and the Machine* (Cambridge, Mass.: MIT Press, 1948).

69. Joseph Schechter, "Bizman Shel Hesster Panim," *Moznayim* 12 (February 1961): 177–181.

70. Yeshurun Keshet, "Al Habikoret Umissaviv La," *Moznayim* 14 (January 1962): 86–87.

71. Avraham Kariv, "Nikreta Ha'olam," *Moznayim* 17 (September-October 1963): 258.

72. Speech by David Levin in the 17th congress of the Teachers' Federation, December 19, 1949, protocol, AJE 9. 160/437, p. 4.

73. See Baruch Ben-Yehuda, "Letoldot Ha'hinuch Be'eretz Israel ad Kom Hamedina." In *Education in Israel,* edited by Haim Ormean (Jerusalem: Ministry of Education, 1973), pp. 1–34 (in Hebrew).

74. Zvi Lam, "Meta'him Ideologi'im—Ma'avakim Al Matrot Ha'hinuch." In ibid., pp. 71–84.

75. Teachers' Federation Pedagogical Committee, "Ikarey Hatoda'ah Hay-ehudit—Israelit Ba'hinuch," a proposal November 3, 1957, AJE 9. 145/382.

76. On the development of the Jewish-consciousness program, see Aharon Kleinberger, *Society, Schools and Progress in Israel* (Oxford: Pergamon, 1969), Chapter 5.

77. Teachers' Federation Pedagogical Committee, protocols of meetings held at the end of 1957 and beginning of 1958, AJE 9. 145/382.

78. See Jerome S. Brunner, *The Process of Education* (Cambridge, Mass.: The President and Fellows of Harvard College, 1960).

79. Aharon Kleinberger, "Hazechut Le'hanech Le'arachim Me'hayvim," *Megamot* 11 (November 1961): 332–337.

80. Hans and Shulamit Kreitler, "The Attitude of Israeli Youth Toward Social Ideals," *Megamot* 13 (August 1964): 174–183 (in Hebrew).

81. Lea Adar and Haim Adler, *Education for Values in Schools for Immigrant Children in Israel* (Jerusalem: The School of Education of the Hebrew University, 1965) (in Hebrew).

82. Hakeness Hapedagogi, protocol, AJE 10. 25/738.

83. Ibid., p. 2.

84. Ibid., p. 20.

85. S. N. Eisenstadt, *Israeli Society* (London: Weidenfeld & Nicolson, 1967), p. 388.

86. S. N. Eisenstadt, "Bureaucracy and Political Development." In *Bureaucracy and Political Development,* edited by Joseph Lapalombara (Princeton, N.J.: Princeton University Press, 1963), p. 118.

87. See S. N. Eisenstadt, Rivkah Bar Yosef, Chaim Adler, eds., *Integration and Development in Israel* (Jerusalem: Israel Universities Press, 1970); and Eva Etzioni-Halevy, *Political Culture in Israel* (New York: Praeger, 1977).

88. See Joseph Ben-David, "Professionals and Unions in Israel," *Industrial Relations* 5 (October 1965): 48–66; Eliezer Tal and Yaron Ezrahi, eds., *Science Policy and Development: The Case of Israel* (New York: Gordon & Breach, 1972); and Prime Minister's Office, National Council for Research and Development, *National Science Policy and Organization of Research in Israel* (Jerusalem: National Council for Research & Development, 1967).

89. On the concept of the "new class," see Alvin W. Gouldner, *The Future of Intellectuals and the Rise of the New Class* (New York: Seabury, 1976); Donald Stabile, *Prophets of Order: The Rise of the New Class, Technocracy and Socialism in America* (Boston, Mass.: South End, 1984); and George Konrád and Ivan Szelényi, *The Intellectuals on the Road to Class Power: A Sociological Study of the Role of the Intelligentsia in Socialism* (New York: Harcourt, Brace, Jovanovich, 1979).

90. Peter Medding, *Mapai in Israel: Political Organization and Government in a New Society* (Cambridge: Cambridge University Press, 1972), Chapter 3.

91. Israel Kessar, "The Changes in the Histadrut's Comprehensiveness," M.A. thesis, Tel Aviv University, 1979 (in Hebrew).

92. A.M., "Ha'academa'im Utenu'at Ha'avoda," *Ovnayim* 3 (1964): 25–33.

93. "Ha'oved Ha'intelectuali Bamedina Utenu'at Ha'avoda," protocol, April 30, 1955, Beit Berl Archives.

94. "Ha'oved Ha'intelectuali: Bema'avakenu lebitahon Ule'atzma'ut Kalkalit," protocol, July 9, 1955, Beit Berl Archives.

95. Ibid., p. 53.

96. "Ha'oved Ha'intelectuali: Bamedina Utenu'at Ha'avoda," p. 94.

97. Comment by S. Blass in "Ha'inteligentzia Utenu'at Hapo'alim," protocol, March 2, 1957, Beit Berl Archives, p. 30.

98. See Alan Arian and Samuel Barnes, "The Dominant Party System: A Neglected Model of Democratic Stability," *Journal of Politics 36* (August 1974): 592–614.

99. On the struggle, see Nathan Yanai, *Qera Batzameret* (Tel Aviv: Levin-Epstein, 1969).

100. *Davar:* "Anshei Ru'ah Matri'im Al Sakana Lademokratia," January 11, 1961.

101. On these beliefs, see, for instance, Benjamin Akzin and Yehezkel Dror, *Israel: High-Pressure Planning* (Syracuse, N.Y.: Syracuse University Press, 1966).

102. For Rafi's point of view, see Gad Yaacobi, *Otzmata Shel Eichut* (Haifa: Shikmona, 1972); and Shimon Peres, *The Next Phase* (Tel Aviv: Am Hassefer, 1965) (in Hebrew).

103. Leonard Fein, *Politics in Israel* (Boston: Little, Brown, 1967), p. 163.

104. Eisenstadt, *Israeli Society,* pp. 351–360.

105. Ibid., p. 360.

# Chapter 4

1. For a collection of Jewish war epics, see *Shirey Milhama Ugevura Be'israel,* edited by Reuven Avinoam and S. Schpaan (Tel Aviv: Maarachot, 1958).

2. Zalman Schneour, "Aspartakus." In ibid., pp. 174–177. See also "Zalman Schneour." In *Pioneers and Builders,* edited by Abraham Goldberg (New York: Abraham Goldberg Publication Committee, 1943), pp. 101–110.

3. On Massada as symbol, see Bernard Lewis, *History—Remembered, Recovered, Invented* (Princeton, N.J.: Princeton University Press, 1975).

4. Haim Gouri, "Bab El-Waad." In *Shirey Milhama Ugevura Be'israel,* edited by Reuven Avinoam and S. Schpaan, p. 369.

5. A. B. Yehoshua, "Facing the Forests." In *Three Days and a Child,* translated by Miriam Arad (Garden City, N.Y.: Doubleday, 1970). See also Nilli Sadan-Loebenstein, *A. B. Yehoshua: Monograph* (Tel Aviv: Sifriat Poalim, 1981) (in Hebrew).

6. Amon Elon, *The Israelis: Founders and Sons* (London: Penguin, 1983).

7. This quotation appeared as a motto in Ronald N. Stromberg, *Redemption by War: The Intellectuals and 1914* (Lawrence: The Regents Press of Kansas, 1982).

8. Gilbert Whittemore, "World War I, Poison Gas Research, and the Ideas of American Chemists," *Social Studies of Science* 5 (1975): 135–163.

9. See Maurice Crosland, "Science and the Franco-Prussian War," *Social Studies of Science* 6 (1976): 185–214.

10. See Carol Gruber, *Mars and Minerva: World War I and the Uses of Higher Learning in America* (Baton Rouge: Louisiana University Press, 1975).

11. See George Frederickson, *The Inner Civil War: Northern Intellectuals and the Crisis of the Union* (New York: Harper & Row, 1965).

12. Randolph S. Bourne, "The War and the Intellectuals." In *War and the Intellectuals: Collected Essays, 1915–1919,* edited by Randolph S. Bourne (New York: Harper & Row, 1964), p. 12.

13. Quoted in Frederickson, p. 66.

14. Quoted in Edward Mead Earle, "H. G. Wells, British Patriot in Search of a World Order." In *Nationalism and Internationalism,* edited by Edward Mead Earle (New York: Columbia University Press, 1950), p. 88.

15. Quoted in ibid., p. 106.

16. H. G. Wells, *The World of William Clissold II* (New York: Doran, 1926), p. 612.

17. Quoted in Earle, p. 106.

18. Bourne, p. 7.

19. Ibid., p. 11.

20. Ibid.

21. Ibid.

22. Gruber.

23. Quoted in ibid., p. 114.

24. Stromberg.

25. Ibid., p. 70.

26. Ralf Dahrendorf, "The Intellectual and Society: The Social Function of the 'Fool' in the Twentieth Century." In *On Intellectuals,* edited by Philip Rieff (Garden City, N.Y.: Doubleday, 1970).

27. On the Six Day War, see Walter Laqueur, *The Road to War* (Middlesex, UK: Penguin Books, 1968); Randolph and Winston Churchill, *The Six Day War* (London: Heinemann, 1967).

28. Moshe Dor, "Ilana'har," *Al Hamishmar,* June 2, 1967.

29. Quoted in Ian Slater, *Orwell: The Road to Airstrip One* (New York: Norton, 1985), p. 171.

30. Dor.

31. R. A., "Amanim Bamilhama," *Haaretz,* June 13, 1967, p. 9.

32. Nathan Zach, "Hashalom Hanitzhi—Be'ikvot Hamilhama," *Haaretz,* June 30, 1976.

33. "Hora'ot Hagara," *Haaretz,* May 28, 1967, p. 8.

34. Aharon Megged, "Beyamin Eleh." *Lamerhav,* May 31, 1967, p. 2.

35. Yossef Harif, "Hashir She'orer Be'hala," *Maariv,* May 19, 1967.

36. Arieh Gilad, letter to the editor, *Haaretz,* June 5, 1967.

37. Meir Verete, letter to the editor, *Haaretz,* May 26, 1967.

38. Bernard Crick, *In Defense of Politics* (Harmondsworth and Middlesex, UK: Penguin, 1964), p. 140.

39. Ehud Ben Ezer, letter to the editor, *Haaretz,* June 2, 1967

40. Nathan Alterman, "Memshelet Herum Ke'hechra'h Elion," *Maariv,* May 26, 1967.

41. Nathan Zach, letter to the editor, *Haaretz,* May 28, 1967.

42. Amos Keynan, letter to the editor, *Haaretz,* May 28, 1967.

43. Professors Unger, Akzin, Guttman, Dror, Zeliger, Czudnowski, Rafaeli, letter to the editor, *Haaretz,* June 2, 1967.

44. Yeshurun Keshet, *In Wartime Jerusalem: Diaries from the Rear* (Jerusalem: Rubin Mass, 1973), p. 215 (in Hebrew).

45. Churchill, p. 55.

46. Laqueur, p. 171.

47. Yehuda Harel, *The Fighter: The Story of General Moshe Dayan* (Tel Aviv: Moked, 1968), pp. 14–15 (in Hebrew).

48. Churchill, p. 60.

49. See Michael Howard, *War in European History* (Oxford: Oxford University Press, 1976); James H. Billington, *Fire in the Minds of Men: Origins of the Revolutionary Faith* (New York: Basic Books, 1980); Ivan Melada, *Guns for Sale: War and Capitalism in English Literature, 1851–1939* (Jefferson, N.C.: McFarland, 1983); Jeffrey Walsh, *American War Literature Nineteen Fourteen to Vietnam* (London: Macmillan, 1982); and Kenneth Waltz, *Man, the State and War* (New York: Columbia University Press, 1954).

50. J. Glenn Gray, *The Warriors: Reflections on Men in Battle* (New York: Harper & Row, 1959), pp. 10–11.

51. Edward Shils, "The Intellectuals and the Powers: Some Perspectives for Comparative Analysis." In *On Intellectuals,* edited by Philip Rieff, p. 27.

52. See Edward Shils, "Intellectuals, Tradition and the Traditions of Intellectuals: Some Preliminary Considerations." In *Intellectuals and Tradition,* edited by S. N. Eisenstadt and S. R. Graubard (New York: Humanities Press, 1973), pp. 27–51.

53. See Gershom Scholem, *The Messianic Idea in Judaism and Other Essays on Jewish Spirituality* (New York: Schocken, 1971).

54. Reported in *Al Hamishmar,* June 16, 1967, p. 5.

55. Israel Eliraz, "Yerushalayim," *Haaretz,* June 16, 1967.

56. Aharon Megged, "Al Har Habayit," *Lamerhav,* June 8, 1967.

57. Aharon Megged, report in *Lamerhav,* June 9, 1967, p. 2.

58. Yeshayahu Leibowitz, interview, *Haaretz,* June 30, 1967, weekly supplement.

59. Moshe Dor, "Be'herdat Levav," *Al Hamishmar,* June 9, 1967.

60. Shulamith Hareven, "Be'har Hazeitim," *Al Hamishmar,* June 30, 1967.

61. R. G. Collingwood, *The New Leviathan* (Oxford: Oxford University Press, 1942), p. 349.

62. Shulamith Hareven, "Ma'hshavot Rishonot," *Al Hamishmar,* June 9, 1967.

63. Shabtai Tevet, "Hatovim Latayis," *Haaretz,* June 20, 1967.

64. Nathan Rotenstreich, personal interview, March 2, 1981.

65. Shmuel Daube, "Ichpat Li O Lo Ichpat Li." *Hed Ha'hinuch* 12 (1967), p. 8.

# Chapter 5

1. *Address by Major-General Yitzhak Rabin* (Jerusalem: Magnes, 1967). The address was given on June 28, 1967.

2. See, for instance, Ladislas Farago, *Patton: Ordeal and Triumph* (New York: Obolensky, 1963).

3. Hillel Weiss, *Portraits of the Fighter: Reflections on Heroes and Heroism in the Hebrew Prose of the Last Decade* (Ramat-Gan: Bar-Ilan University, 1975), p. 17 (in Hebrew).

4. See Martin Buber, *To Hallow This Life: An Anthology,* edited by Jacob Trapp (New York: Harper, 1958).

5. See Karl Deutsch, *The Nerves of Government* (New York: Free Press, 1966).

6. See Zvi Lanir, *Fundamental Surprise* (Eugene, Oreg.: Decision Research, 1986).

7. For an interesting exception, see Carl Frankenstein, "Political Crisis and Education." In *In the Aftermath of the Yom Kippur War,* edited by Adir Cohen and Ephrat Carmon (Haifa: Haifa University, 1976), pp. 15–30 (in Hebrew).

8. See Zvi Lanir, "Academic Research and National Misconceptions," *Jerusalem Quarterly* 32 (Summer 1984): 36–47.

9. Dan Miron, "Te'uda Be'israel," undated, distributed to subscribers of *Politika,* 1988, p. 14.

10. C. P. Snow, *Science and Government* (London: Oxford University Press, 1960).

11. Geula Cohen, "Hashulhan Hameruba," *Maariv,* November 18, 1966.

12. Gershon Bergson, "Ma'assim Bahinuch Le'ahar Hamilhama," *Hed Hahinuch* 13 (1968): 7.

13. Zvi Galon in a symposium on the educational meaning of the war, held on December 6, 1967, published as a booklet by The Education Society, Haifa, 1969.

14. See Michael Keren, "Criteria for the Evaluation of Secure Borders," *Research Project: Criteria for Defining Secure Borders* (Tel Aviv: Tel Aviv University, Center for Strategic Studies, 1978).

15. Mordecai Kashtan and Eithan Haber, *Thus We Won* (Tel Aviv: Nativ, 1967), p. 53 (in Hebrew).

16. Yehuda Walach, "Eich Ninhag Bayom Hashevi'i," *Keshet* 38 (Winter 1968): 110.

17. Ibid.

18. Moshe Atar, "Ketz La'agadot," *Keshet* 38 (Winter 1968): 105.

19. Haim Gouri, *Dapim Yerushalmi'im* (Tel Aviv: Hakkibutz Hameuhad, 1968), p. 291.

20. Atar, p. 104.

21. Amnon Rubinstein, "Ma Ya'asse Hazeman?" *Haaretz,* July 10, 1967.

22. Yael Dayan, *A Soldier's Diary: Sinai 1967* (London: Weidenfeld and Nicolson, 1967).

23. See Haim Be'er, "'Hashalom Ha'ivri' shel Yonatan Ratosh," *Haaretz,* October 27, 1967.

24. Haim Be'er, "Mehir Hashalom Ufri Hameta'h Habithoni," *Haaretz,* July 14, 1967.

25. Avraham Raz, "Mehir Hashalom Ufri Hameta'h Habithoni," *Haaretz,* July 21, 1967.

26. See discussion on this point in Amos Elon, *The Israelis: Founders and Sons* (London: Penguin, 1983).

27. Quoted in Be'er.

28. Yehoshua Palmon, "Im Mi Me'ha'arvim Nadun?" *Haaretz,* September 28, 1967.

29. Nathan Yellin Mor, "Eretz Ahat Lishney Amim," *Haaretz,* October 3, 1967.

30. Shlomo Avinery, "Israel Veki'yum Mamlechet Yarden," *Haaretz,* March 22, 1968.

31. Ibid.

32. Ibid.

33. Ibid.

34. The debate was published in *Be'ad Veneged* 37 (January 1970): 17–27.

35. Ofira Seliktar, *New Zionism and the Foreign Policy System of Israel* (London: Croom Helm, 1986).

36. On Israel after 1967, see Robert Freedman, ed., *Israel in the Begin Era* (New York: Praeger, 1982); Charles Liebman and Eliezer Don Yehiya, *Civil Religion in Israel* (Berkeley: University of California Press, 1983); and Shmuel Sandler and Hillel Frisch, *Israel, the Palestinians and the West Bank* (Lexington, Mass.: Heath, 1984).

37. See Chapter 1.

38. See J. L. Talmon, *Political Messianism: The Romantic Phase* (New York: Praeger, 1960).

39. S. Yizhar, "Al Meshorerey Hassipua'h," *Haaretz,* December 8, 1967.

40. J. L. Talmon, "Israel Among the Nations: The Six Day War in Historical Perspective." In *Israel Among the Nations,* edited by J. L. Talmon (London: Weidenfeld & Nicolson, 1970, pp. 180–181.

41. Ibid., p. 181.

42. Ibid.

43. See, for example, Yaacov Chasdai, *Truth in the Shadow of War* (Tel Aviv: Zmora, Bitan, Modan, 1978) (in Hebrew).

44. Amos Oz, *In the Land of Israel* (New York: Harcourt, Brace, Jovanovich, 1983), p. 134.

45. Amos Oz, *A Perfect Peace* (Tel Aviv: Am Oved, 1982) (in Hebrew).

46. Oz, *In the Land of Israel,* p. 139.

47. Ibid.

48. Ibid., p. 130.

49. Yaacov Shavit, quoted in Y. Harkabi, *Fateful Decisions* (Tel Aviv: Am Oved, 1986), p. 125 (in Hebrew).

50. See Michael Keren, "Ben-Gurion and the Intellectuals," *Forum* 57-58 (Winter-Spring 85/86): 7–15.

51. See, for instance, Asher Maniv, *The Weakness of Force* (Tel Aviv: Hakibbutz Hameuchad, 1987) (in Hebrew).

52. Amnon Rubinstein, *The Zionist Dream Revisited: From Herzl to Gush Emunim and Back* (New York: Schocken, 1984).

53. From *The Bar-Kokhba Syndrome,* quoted in Howard M. Sachar, *A History of Israel: From the Aftermath of the Yom Kippur War* (New York: Oxford University Press, 1987), p. 256.

54. Mordechai Kremnizer, "Academia Mishpatit Lo'hemet." In *The Deadlock Years—Personal Witness,* edited by Arye Palgi (Tel Aviv: Sifriat Poalim, 1988), pp. 50–52 (in Hebrew).

55. Shulamith Hareven, "Tafkid Ha'intelectual." In *Messiah Or Knesset,* edited by Shulamith Hareven (Tel Aviv: Zmora, Bitan, 1987), pp. 101–109 (in Hebrew).

56. Aharon Megged, *The Turbulent Zone* (Tel Aviv: Hakibbutz Hameuchad, 1985) (in Hebrew).

57. See Miron Benvenisti, *The Sling and the Club* (Jerusalem: Keter, 1988).

58. Saul Friedlander, *When Memory Comes* (New York: Avon, 1978).

59. Gershon Shaked, "Ein Makom A'her." In *No Other Place: On Literature and Society* (Tel Aviv: Hakibbutz Hameuchad, 1983) (in Hebrew).

# Index